Careers in Focus

Environment

Ferguson Publishing Company
Chicago, Illinois

Copyright © 1999 Ferguson Publishing Company
ISBN 0-89434-288-6

Library of Congress Cataloging-in-Publication Data

Careers in focus.   Environment.—2nd ed.
        p.   cm.
    Includes index.
    ISBN 0-89434-288-6
        1. Environmental sciences—Vocational guidance—United States—
Handbooks, manuals, etc. 2. Environmentalists—Vocational guidance—
United States—Handbooks, manuals, etc. 3. Environmental engineering—
Vocational guidance—United States—Handbooks, manuals, etc.   4.
Environmental   engineers—Vocational   guidance—United   States—
Handbooks, manuals, etc. I. J.G. Ferguson Publishing Company. II. Title:
Environment.
GE60.C39   1999   99-36431
363.7'0023'73—dc21   CIP

Printed in the United States of America

Cover photo courtesy Joseph Sohn/Tony Stone Images

Published and distributed by
Ferguson Publishing Company
200 West Jackson Boulevard, 7th Floor
Chicago, Illinois 60606
312-692-1000

Y - 6

Table of Contents

Introduction

The Environmental Careers Organization (ECO) breaks down environmental careers into these broad categories: parks and outdoor recreation, air and water quality management, education and communication, hazardous waste management, land and water conservation, fishery and wildlife management, forestry, planning, and solid waste management. What's more, says ECO, new kinds of jobs are being created all the time to meet new demands. There currently are more than 30 major environment-related areas of study at the college level, and some experts say that we've only begun to see the tip of the iceberg in terms of types of environmental jobs.

Because of growing concern in the United States and around the world for the future health and survival of the planet, most indicators point to a large growth in the field of environmental sciences. Exactly how large is difficult to project because the amount of attention paid to the environment in this country varies with each political administration and other issues, such as the health of the economy and the tension between creating new jobs and protecting the environment. Media attention to one cause or another, such as preserving the wetlands, saving the rain forests, saving the whales, or recycling, waxes and wanes. Even so, the media helps to periodically remind people that significant environmental problems urgently need answers.

Another factor in favor of environmental cleanup is the waning of the nuclear arms race. Industrialized nations now have more resources to find alternatives to fossil fuels, protect the ozone layer, put a stop to habitat and species destruction, and develop methods for conserving water, energy, and other resources.

In the United States, spending on the environment has risen from $30 billion in 1972 to an estimated $295 billion in 1998. The environmental industry as a whole is growing more slowly now than in the past—from 16 to 30 percent per year in the middle to late 1980s to about 4 percent in 1992, and a projected 5 to 7 percent for the next 5 years. *Environmental Business Journal* says there were 793,159 environmental jobs in 1988, 1,073,397 in 1992, and 1,327,150 in 1997.

Each article in this book discusses a particular environmental occupation in detail. The information comes from Ferguson's *Encyclopedia of Careers and Vocational Guidance*. The History section describes the history of the particular job as it relates to the overall development of its industry or field. The Job describes the primary and secondary duties of the job. Requirements discusses high school and postsecondary education and training requirements, any certification or licensing necessary, and any other personal requirements for success in the job. Exploring offers suggestions on how to gain some experience in or knowledge of the particular job before making a firm educational and financial commitment. The focus is on what can be done while still in high school (or in the early years of college) to gain a better understanding of the job. The Employers section gives an overview of typical places of employment for the job. Starting Out discusses the best ways to land that first job, be it through the college placement office, newspaper ads, or personal contact. The Advancement section describes what kind of career path to expect from the job and how to get there. Earnings lists salary ranges and describes the typical fringe benefits. The Work Environment section describes the typical surroundings and conditions of employment—whether indoors or outdoors, noisy or quiet, social or independent, and so on. Also discussed are typical hours worked, any seasonal fluctuations, and the stresses and strains of the job. The Outlook section summarizes the job in terms of the general economy and industry projections. For the most part, Outlook information is obtained from the Bureau of Labor Statistics and is supplemented by information taken from professional associations. Job growth terms follow those used in the Occupational Outlook Handbook: Growth described as "much faster than the average" means an increase of 36 percent or more. Growth described as "faster than the average" means an increase of 21 to 35 percent. Growth described as "about as fast as the average" means an increase of 10 to 20 percent. Growth described as "little change or more slowly than the average" means an increase of 0 to 9 percent. "Decline" means a decrease of 1 percent or more.

Each article ends with For More Information, which lists organizations that can provide career information on training, education, internships, scholarships, and job placement.

Air Quality Engineers

School Subjects

Biology
Chemistry
Mathematics

Personal Skills

Communication/ideas
Technical/scientific

Work Environment

Primarily indoors
Primarily one location

Minimum Education Level

Bachelor's degree

Salary Range

$23,000 to $35,000 to $70,000+

Certification or Licensing

Voluntary

Outlook

Faster than the average

Overview

Air quality engineers, or *air pollution control engineers,* are responsible for developing techniques to analyze and control air pollution by using sophisticated monitoring, chemical analysis, computer modeling, and statistical analysis. Some air quality engineers are involved in pollution-control equipment design or modification. Government-employed air quality experts keep track of a region's polluters, enforce federal regulations, and impose fines or take other action against those who do not comply with regulations. Privately employed engineers may monitor companies' emissions for certain targeted pollutants to ensure that they are within acceptable levels. Air quality engineers who work in research seek ways to combat or avoid air pollution.

History

The growth of cities during the Industrial Revolution was a major contributor to the decline of air quality. Some contaminates (pollutants) have always been with us—for instance, particulate matter (tiny solid particles) from very large fires or dust caused by wind or mass animal migration. But human populations were not really concentrated enough, nor did the technology exist to produce what is today considered hazardous to the atmosphere, until about 200 years ago. The industrialization of England in the 1750s, followed by France in the 1830s and Germany in the 1850s, changed all that. It created high-density populations as thousands of people were drawn to cities to work in the smoke-belching factories and led to huge increases in airborne pollutants. Work conditions in the factories were notoriously bad, with no pollution-control or safety measures. Rapidly, living conditions in cities became equally bad; the air became severely polluted air and caused respiratory and other diseases.

America's cities were slightly smaller and slower to industrialize, in addition to being more spread out than Old World capitals like London. Even so, levels of sulfur dioxide were so high in Pittsburgh in the early 1900s that ladies' stockings would disintegrate upon prolonged exposure to the air. The rapid growth of the American automobile industry in the first half of the 20th century contributed greatly to air pollution in two ways: initially, from the steel factories and production plants that made economic giants out of places like Pittsburgh and Detroit, and then from the cars themselves. This became an even greater problem as cars enabled people to move out from the fetid industrial city and commute to work there. Mobility independent of public transportation greatly increased auto exhaust and created such modern nightmares as rush hour traffic.

The effects of air pollution were and are numerous. Particulate matter reacts chemically with heat to form ground-level ozone, or smog. Sulfur and nitrogen oxides cause extensive property damage over long periods with their corrosive qualities. Carbon monoxide, the main automobile pollutant, is deadly at a relatively low level of exposure.

According to data from the Environmental Careers Organization, 88 percent of carbon dioxide measured in the Los Angeles basin and 50 percent of that region's volatile organics (a cause of ozone smog) were the result of automobile emissions. This was true despite the Los Angeles basin's having the toughest vehicle emission standards in the United States and the largest market for alternative energy source automobiles. Air pollution affects the environment in well-publicized phenomena like acid rain and holes in the ozone layer, and in less obvious ways as well. For example, a scientist in Great Britain at the turn of the 20th century followed the evolution of white tree moths as natural selection turned them gray to match the birch trees they used for camouflage, which had become covered with a layer of airborne industrial pollutants. Because pollution is so difficult to remove from the air, and because its effects (loss of atmospheric ozone, for example) are so difficult to alter, the problem tends to be cumulative and an increasingly critical public health issue.

Some private air pollution control was implemented in the 20th century, mainly to prevent factories from ruining their own works with corrosive (strongly acid or caustic) and unhealthy emissions. The first attempt at governmental regulation was the Clean Air Act (1955), but because environmental concerns were not considered viable economic or political issues, this act was not very effective. As environmentalists became increasingly visible and vigorous campaigners, the Air Quality Act was established in 1967. The Environmental Protection Agency (EPA) created National Ambient Air Quality Standards (NAAQS) in 1971, which set limits on ozone, carbon monoxide, sulfur dioxide, lead, nitrogen dioxide, and particulate levels in the emissions of certain industries and processes. States were supposed to design and implement plans to meet the NAAQS, but so few complied that Congress was forced to extend deadlines three times. Even now, many goals set by the first generation of air-quality regulations remain unmet, and new pollution issues demand attention. Airborne toxins, indoor air pollution, acid rain, carbon dioxide buildup (the greenhouse effect), and depletion of the ozone are now subjects of international controversy and concern.

The Job

The EPA has composed a list of more than 50 regions of the United States that are out of compliance with federal air quality regulations—some dramatically so—and provided deadlines within the next 20 years to bring these areas under control. The EPA regulations cover everything from car emissions to the greenhouse effect and have the weight of law behind them. There are few industries that will not be touched somehow by this legislation and few that will not require the services of an air quality engineer in the years to come.

Air quality engineers will be the professionals monitoring targeted industries or sources to determine whether they are operating within acceptable emissions levels. These engineers will suggest changes in the setup of specific companies, or even whole industries, to lessen their impact on the atmosphere. There will be ample opportunity in this field to combine interests, precisely because it is a new field with yet unestablished job paths. An air quality engineer with some background in meteorology, for example, might track the spread of airborne pollutants through various weather systems, using computer modeling techniques. Another air quality engineer might research indoor air pollution, discovering causes for the "sick building syndrome" and creating new architectural standards and building codes for safe ventilation and construction materials.

Air quality engineers work for the government, in private industry, as consultants, and in research and development. Government employees are responsible for monitoring a region, citing infractions, and otherwise enforcing government regulations. These workers may be called to give testimony in cases against noncompliant companies. They must deal with public concerns and opinion and are themselves regulated by government bureaucracy and regulations.

Air quality engineers in private industry work within industry or a large company to ensure that air quality regulations are being met. They might be responsible for developing instrumentation to continuously monitor emissions, for example, and using this data to formulate methods of control. They may interact with federal regulators or work independently. Engineers working in private industry also might be involved in what is known as "impact assessment with the goal of sustainable development." This means figuring out the most environmentally sound way to produce products—from raw material to disposal stages—while maintaining or, if possible, increasing the company's profits.

Engineers who work alone as consultants or for consulting firms do many of the same things as engineers in private industry, perhaps for smaller companies that do not need a full-time engineer but still need help meeting federal requirements. They, too, might suggest changes to be implemented by a company to reduce air pollution. Some consultants specialize in certain areas of pollution control. Selling, installing, and running a particular control system is the business of many private consultants. The job requires some salesmanship and the motivation to maintain a variable clientele.

Finally, engineers committed to research and development may work in public or private research institutions and in academic environments. They may tackle significant problems that affect any number of industries and may improve air quality standards with the discovery of new contaminates that need regulation.

Requirements

High School

High school students should develop their skills in chemistry, math, biology, and ecology.

Postsecondary Training

To break into this field, a bachelor's degree in civil, environmental, or chemical engineering is required. Advancement, specialization, or jobs in research may require a master's degree or Ph.D. Besides the regular environmental or chemical engineering curricula at the college level, future air quality engineers might engage in some mechanical or civil engineering if they are interested in product development. Modelers and planners should have a good knowledge of computer systems. Supporting course work in biology, toxicology, or meteorology can give the job seeker an edge for certain specialized positions even before the individual gains experience in the workforce.

Certification or Licensing

All engineers who do work that affects public health, safety, or property must register with the state. To obtain registration, engineers must have a degree from an accredited engineering program. Right before they get their degree (or soon after), they must pass an engineer-in-training (EIT) exam covering fundamentals of science and engineering. A few years into their careers, engineers also must pass an exam covering engineering practice.

Other Requirements

Prospective air quality engineers should be puzzle solvers. The ability to work with intangibles is a trait of successful air quality management. As in most fields nowadays, communications skills are vital. Engineers must be able to clearly communicate their ideas and findings, both orally and in writing, to a variety of people with different levels of technical understanding.

Exploring

Investigating air quality engineering can begin with reading environmental science and engineering periodicals, available in many large libraries. Familiarizing yourself with the current issues involving air pollution will give you a better idea of what problems will be facing this field in the near future.

The next step might be a call to a local branch of the EPA. In addition to providing information about local source problems, the EPA can also provide a breakdown of air quality standards that must be met and who has to meet them.

To get a better idea about college-level course work and possible career directions, contact major universities, environmental associations, or even private environmental firms. Some private consulting firms will explain how specific areas of study combine to create their particular area of expertise.

Employers

Most air quality engineers are privately employed in industries subject to emissions control, such as manufacturing. They may also work for the federal government investigating and ensuring compliance with air quality regulations, as consultants to industry and large companies, and in research and development.

Starting Out

A summer position as an air pollution technician provides valuable insight into the engineer's job as well as contacts and experience. Check with local and state EPA offices and larger consulting firms in your area for internship positions and their requirements. Environmentally oriented engineers may be able to volunteer for citizen watchdog group monitoring programs and patrol regions for previously undiscovered or unregulated contaminates. Most air quality engineers can expect to get jobs in their field immediately after graduating with a bachelor's degree. Your school placement office can assist you in fine-tuning your resume and setting up interviews with potential employers. Government positions are a common point of entry; high turnover rates open positions as experienced engineers leave for the more lucrative private sector, which accounts for four out of five jobs in air quality management. An entry-level job might focus on monitoring and analysis.

Advancement

With experience and education, the engineer might develop a specialization within the field of air quality. Research grants are sometimes available to experienced engineers who wish to concentrate on specific problems or areas of study. Management is another avenue of advancement. The demand for technically oriented middle management in the private sector makes engineers with good interpersonal skills very valuable.

In many ways, advancement will be dictated by the increasing value of air quality engineers to business and industry in general. Successful development of air pollution control equipment or systems—perhaps that even cut costs as they reduce pollution—will make air quality engineers important players in companies' economic strategies. As regulations tighten and increasing emphasis is put on minimizing environmental impact, air quality engineers will be in the spotlight as both regulators and innovators. Advancement may come in the form of monetary incentives or bonuses or management positions over other parts of the organization or company.

Earnings

According to *Engineering News Record*, an estimated $95 billion in revenue will result from growth in this field in the next 20 years. Job opportunities through the next decade will be high, probably higher in those areas of the country targeted by the EPA (generally, larger cities like Los Angeles, Chicago, and Denver). Salaries for entry-level engineers start at around $23,000 to $35,000 per year. Local government agencies pay at the lower end of the scale; state and federal agencies, slightly higher. Salaries in the private sector are highest, from the low $30,000s up to $70,000 or more. Other benefits may include tuition reimbursement programs, use of a company vehicle for fieldwork, full health coverage, retirement plans, and fairly solid job security.

Work Environment

Working conditions differ depending on the employer, the specialization of the position, and the location of the job. An air quality engineer may be required to perform fieldwork, such as observing emission sources, but more often works in an office, determining the factors responsible for airborne pollutants and devising ways to prevent them. Co-workers may include other environmental engineers, lab technicians, and office personnel. An engineer may discuss specific problems with a company's economic planners and develop programs to make that company more competitive environmentally and economically. Those who monitor emissions have considerable responsibility and therefore considerable pressure to do their job well—failure to maintain industry standards could cost their employers government fines. Engineers in some consulting firms may be required to help sell the system they develop or work use.

Most engineers work a standard 40-hour week, putting in overtime to solve critical problems as quickly as possible. A large part of the job for most air quality engineers consists of keeping up-to-date with federal regulations, industry and regional standards, and developments in their areas of expertise. Some employers require standard business attire, while some require more fieldwork from their engineers and may not enforce rigorous dress codes. Unlike water and soil pollution, air pollution can sometimes be difficult to measure quantitatively if the source is unknown. Major pollutants are generally easily identified (although not so easily eliminated), but traces of small "leaks" may literally change with the wind and make for time-consuming, deliberate, and frustrating work.

Outlook

When the immediate scramble to modify and monitor equipment slackens as government regulations are met in the next 20 years, the focus in air quality engineering will shift from traditional "end of pipe" controls (e.g., modifying catalytic converters or gasoline to make cars burn gas more cleanly) to source control (developing alternative fuels and eliminating oil-based industrial emissions). As mentioned, impact assessment will play a large part on the corporate side of air quality management, as businesses strive to stay profitable in the wake of public health and safety regulations. Air pollution problems like greenhouse gas buildup and ozone pollution will not be disappearing in the near future and will be increasingly vital areas of research.

International development will allow American pollution control engineers to offer their services in any part of the world that has growing industries or population. Pollution control in general has a big future: air pollution control is quickly becoming a major chunk of the expected expenditures and revenues in this category.

For More Information

The following organization's members work in air pollution control and hazardous waste management:

Air and Waste Management Association
One Gateway Center, Third Floor
Pittsburgh, PA 15222
Tel: 412-232-3444
Email: info@awma.org
Web: http://www.awma.org

The following are government pollution control boards:

State and Territorial Air Pollution Program Administrators (STAPPA) and the Association of Local Air Pollution Control Officials (ALAPCO)
444 North Capitol Street, NW, Suite 307
Washington, DC 20001
Tel: 202-624-7864
Email: 4clnair@sso.org
Web: http://www.4cleanair.org/

Following is the national organization. For your state's Environmental Protection Agency, check the government listings in your phone book:

Environmental Protection Agency
401 M Street, SW
Washington, DC 20460-0003
Tel: 202-260-2090
Web: http://www.epa.gov

Ecologists

Biology Chemistry	School Subjects
Communication/ideas Technical/scientific	Personal Skills
Primarily outdoors Primarily multiple locations	Work Environment
Bachelor's degree	Minimum Education Level
$10,000 to $45,000 to $175,000+	Salary Range
None available	Certification or Licensing
Faster than the average	Outlook

Overview

Ecology is the study of the interconnections between organisms (plants, animals) and the physical environment. It links biology, which includes both zoology (the study of animals) and botany (the study of plants), with physical sciences, such as geology and paleontology. Thus, *ecologist* is a broad name for any of a number of different biological or physical scientists concerned with the study of plants or animals within their environment.

History

Much of the science that ecologists use is not new. The ancient Greeks recorded their observations of natural history many centuries ago. However, linking together the studies of life and the physical environment is fairly new. The term "ecology" was first defined in 1866 by Ernst von Haeckel (1834-1919), a German biologist. Like many scientists of his time, he grappled with Charles Darwin's (1809-82) theory of evolution based on natural selection. This theory said that those species of plants and animals that were best adapted to their environment would survive. Although Haeckel did not agree with Darwin, he and many other scientists grew fascinated with the links between living things and their physical environment. At that time, very important discoveries in geology proved that many forms of plants and animals had once existed but had died out. Fossils showed startlingly unfamiliar plant types, for example, as well as prehistoric animal remains that no one had ever imagined existed. (Before such discoveries, people assumed that the species they saw all around them had always existed.) Realization that there were important connections between living things and their physical environment was a key step in the development of the science of ecology.

Like most of the other environmental careers, the professional field of ecology did not really grow popular until the late 1960s and early 1970s. Before then, some scientists and others had tried to warn the public about the ill effects of industrialization, unchecked natural resource consumption, overpopulation, spoiling of wilderness areas, and other thoughtless misuse of the environment. But not until the years after World War II—with growing use of radiation and of pesticides and other chemicals, soaring industrial and automobile pollution, and increasing discharge into waterways—did widespread public alarm about the environment grow. By this time, many feared it was too late. Heavy municipal and industrial discharge into Lake Erie, for example, made it unable to sustain life as before.

In response, the U.S. government passed a series of hard-hitting environmental laws through the 1960s and 1970s. To become compliant with these laws, companies and municipalities began to look around for professionals who understood the problems and could help take steps to remedy them. Originally, they drew professionals from many existing fields—geologists, sanitary engineers, biologists, chemists, and others. These professionals may not have studied environmental problems as such at school, but they were able to apply the science they knew to the problems at hand.

To some extent, this continues to be true today. Many people working on environmental problems still come out of general science or engineering backgrounds. The 1990s, however, brought about a trend toward specialization. Students in many fields—from biology and chemistry to engineering, law, urban planning, communications, and others—can obtain degrees with specialization in the environment. An ecologist today can either have a background in traditional biological or physical sciences or have studied these subjects specifically in the context of environmental problems.

The Job

The main unit of study in ecology is the ecosystem. *Ecosystems* are communities of plants and animals within a given habitat that provide the necessary means of survival, including food and water. Ecosystems are defined by such physical conditions as climate, altitude, latitude, soil and water characteristics, and so forth. Examples include forests, tundra, savannas (grasslands), and rainforests, among others.

There are many complex and delicate interrelationships within an ecosystem. For example, green plants use the energy of sunlight to make carbohydrates, fats, and proteins; some animals eat these plants and acquire part of the energy of the carbohydrates, fats, and proteins; other animals eat these animals and acquire a smaller part of that energy. Cycles of photosynthesis, respiration, and nitrogen fixation continuously recycle the chemicals of life needed to support the ecosystem. Anything that disrupts these cycles—from droughts to air or water pollution—can disrupt the delicate workings of the entire ecosystem.

Therefore, a primary concern of ecologists today is to study and attempt to find solutions for disruptions in various ecosystems. Increasingly, an area of expertise is the reconstruction of ecosystems—that is, the re-creation of ecosystems that are destroyed or almost completely destroyed because of pollution, overuse of land, or other action.

According to the Environmental Careers Organization (ECO), a key area of work for ecologists is in land and water conservation. They help to restore damaged land and water as well as to preserve wild areas for the future. Understanding the links between organisms and their physical environments can be invaluable in such efforts.

Let's take an example to see how this works. Imagine that there is a large pond at the edge of a town. A woman out jogging one day notices that hundreds of small, dead fish have washed up at the edge of the pond—a "fish kill," in environmental language. Clearly, something is wrong: but what? A nearby factory discharges its wastewater into the pond. Is there something new in the wastewater that killed the fish? Or did something else kill the fish? A professional who understands the fish, the habitat (the pond), the possible reasons for the fish kill, and the potential solutions clearly would be useful here.

This is also true for environmental planning and resource management. Planning involves studying and reporting the impact of an action on the environment—for example, how the construction of a new federal highway may affect the surrounding ecosystem. A planning team may go to the site to view the physical geography and environment, the plants, and the animals.

It also may recommend alternative actions that will have less damaging effects.

Resource management means determining what resources already exist and working to use them wisely. Professionals may build databases cataloging the plants, animals, and physical characteristics of a given area. They also may report on what can be done to ensure that the ecosystem can sustain itself in the future. If an ecosystem has been completely destroyed, ecologists can help reconstruct it, getting the physical environment back up to par and reintroducing the species that used to live there.

Requirements

High School

If you are interested in becoming an ecologist, you should take science, biology, earth science, English, and math courses in high school.

Postsecondary Training

A bachelor of science degree is the minimum requirement for nonresearch jobs, which include testing and inspection. A master's degree is necessary for jobs in applied research or management. A Ph.D. generally is required to advance in the field, including into administrative positions.

ECO says that if you can only take one undergraduate major, it should be in the basic sciences: biology, botany, zoology, chemistry, physics, or geology. ECO adds that, at the master's degree level, natural resource management, ecology, botany, conservation biology, and forestry studies are useful.

There are many areas of specialization. *Limnologists* study freshwater ecology; *hydrogeologists* focus on water on or below the surface of the earth; *paleontologists* study the remains of ancient life-forms in the form of fossils; *geomorphologists* study the origin of landforms and their changes; and *geochemists* study the chemistry of the earth, including the effect of pollution on the earth's chemistry. Other specialties are those of the endangered species biologists and wetlands ecologists.

Other Requirements

Ecologists should appreciate and respect nature, and they must also be well versed in scientific fundamentals. Ecologists frequently, but not always, are naturally idealistic. They should be able to work with other people on a team and to express their special knowledge to the other people on the team, who may have different areas of specialization.

Exploring

You can seek more information about ecology from guidance counselors and professional ecologists who work at nearby colleges, universities, and government agencies. An easy way for you to learn more about ecology is to study your own environment. Trips to a nearby pond, forest, or park over the course of several months will provide opportunities to observe and collect data. Science teachers and local park service or arboretum personnel can also offer you guidance.

Employers

By far the majority of land and water conservation jobs—about 75 percent— are in the public sector, according to ECO. This includes the federal government, the largest employer. The Bureau of Land Management, the U.S. Fish and Wildlife Service, the National Park Service, and the U.S. Geological Service are among the federal agencies who manage U.S. conservation. Other public sector opportunities are with states, regions, and towns. Opportunities in the private sector can be found with utilities, timber companies, and consulting firms, according to ECO. An additional area of employment is in teaching.

Starting Out

You should volunteer with such groups as the Student Conservation Association (SCA), which places people in resource management projects. Programs include three- to five-week summer internships for high school students. If you have already graduated from high school (and are over age 18), you can check with SCA for internships in forest, wildlife, resource, and other agencies.

Another option is to contact a federal or local government agency directly about an internship. Many, including the EPA, National Park Service, and Bureau of Land Management, have internship programs. Programs are more informal at the local level.

As for the private sector, an internship with a nonprofit organization may be possible. Such groups include the National Wildlife Federation and the Natural Resources Defense Council.

Entry-level ecologists also may take advantage of temporary or seasonal jobs.

Advancement

Midlevel biological scientists may move to managerial positions within biology or to nontechnical administrative, sales, or managerial jobs. Ecologists with a Ph.D. may conduct independent research, advance into administrative positions, or teach on the college level, advancing from assistant professor to associate and tenured professorships.

Earnings

According to the Ecological Society of America, salaries for ecologists can range from $10,000 per year to $175,000 and above. Salaries of $175,000 and above are quite rare, however—most experienced and successful ecologists in academia and government can hope to earn salaries of no more than $85,000. The median income for ecologists is about $45,000.

Federal agency jobs tend to pay more than state or local agency jobs. Private sector jobs tend to pay more than public sector jobs.

Work Environment

A job in ecology can take you outdoors—to a wilderness area, a forest, a mountain stream. Ecologists also might work in sewage treatment plants, spend their days in front of computers or in research laboratories, or find themselves testifying in court. A certain amount of idealism probably is useful, though not required. It takes more than just loving nature to be in this field—a person has to be good at scientific fundamentals. Ecologists might start out in the field collecting samples, making notes about animal habits, or doing other monitoring. They may need to be able to work as part of a team and express what they know in terms that everyone on the team can understand.

Outlook

Environmentally oriented jobs are expected to increase at a faster rate than the average for all occupations through 2006, according to the U.S. Department of Labor. Land and resource conservation jobs tend to be the most scarce, however, because of high popularity and tight budgets for agencies. Those with advanced degrees will fare better than ecologists with only bachelor's degrees.

For More Information

For information on careers in the geosciences, contact:

American Geological Institute
4220 King Street
Alexandria, VA 22302-1502
Tel: 703-379-2480
Email: agi@agiweb.org
Web: http://www.agiweb.org

National Wildlife Federation
8925 Leesburg Pike
Vienna, VA 22184
Tel: 703-790-4000
Web: http://www.nwf.org

ESA offers a wide variety of career publications, including electronic versions of its brochures, Careers in Ecology, Focus on Ecologists, *and* What Does Ecology Have to Do with Me?, *at its Web site. For more information contact:*

Ecological Society of America
2010 Massachusetts Avenue, NW, Suite 400
Washington, DC 20036
Tel: 202-833-8773
Email: esahq@esa.org
Web: http://www.sdsc.edu/projects/ESA/esa.htm

For information on student volunteer activities and programs, contact:

Student Conservation Association
689 River Road
PO Box 550
Charlestown, NH 03603-0550
Tel: 603-543-1700
Web: http://www.sca-inc.org

Energy Conservation Technicians

Mathematics Physics	School Subjects
Helping/teaching Mechanical/manipulative	Personal Skills
Indoors and outdoors Primarily multiple locations	Work Environment
High school diploma	Minimum Education Level
$12,000 to $35,000 to $58,000	Salary Range
Voluntary	Certification or Licensing
About as fast as the average	Outlook

Overview

Energy conservation technicians identify and measure the amount of energy used to heat, cool, and operate a facility or industrial process. They assess the efficiency of energy use and determine the amount of energy lost through wasteful processes or lack of insulation. They also suggest energy conservation techniques.

History

At the start of the 20th century, energy costs were only a small part of the expense of operating homes, offices, and factories and of providing lighting, communication, and transportation. Coal and petroleum were abundant and relatively inexpensive. Low energy prices contributed to the emergence of the United States as the leading industrialized nation in the world and as the world's largest energy consumer. Because petroleum was inexpensive and could easily produce heat, steam, electricity, and fuel, it displaced coal for many purposes. As a result, the nation's coal-mining industry declined, and the United States became dependent on foreign oil for half of its energy supply.

In 1973, when many foreign oil-producing nations stopped shipments of oil to the United States and other Western countries, fuel costs increased dramatically. Although increased domestic oil production and decreased reliance on imports have since resulted in more stable prices, uncertainty about imported energy supplies remains. This uncertainty and a growing awareness about environmental pollution have fueled the development of energy conservation techniques in the United States. The emphasis on discovering new sources of energy, developing more efficient methods and equipment to use energy, and reducing the amount of wasted energy has created a demand for energy conservation technicians.

The Job

Energy efficiency and conservation are major concerns in nearly all homes and workplaces. This means that job settings and work assignments for energy conservation technicians vary greatly. They may inspect homes, businesses, and industrial buildings to identify conditions that cause energy waste, recommend ways to reduce the waste, and help install corrective measures. They may be employed in power plants, research laboratories, construction firms, industrial facilities, government agencies, or companies that sell and service equipment. The jobs these technicians perform can be divided into four major areas of energy activity: research and development, production, use, and conservation.

In research and development, technicians usually work in laboratories testing mechanical, electrical, chemical, pneumatic, hydraulic, thermal, or optical scientific principles. Typical employers include institutions, private industry, government, and the military. Working under the direction of an engineer, physicist, chemist, or metallurgist, technicians use specialized equipment and materials to perform laboratory experiments. They help record data and analyze it using computers. They may also be responsible for periodic maintenance and repair of equipment.

In energy production, typical employers include solar energy equipment manufacturers, installers, and users; power plants; and process plants that use high-temperature heat, steam, or hot water. Technicians in this field work with engineers and managers to develop, install, operate, maintain, modify, and repair systems and devices used for the conversion of fuels or other resources into useful energy. Such plants may produce hot water, steam, mechanical motion, or electrical power; typical systems include furnaces, electrical power plants, and solar heating systems. These systems may be controlled manually by semiautomated control panels or by computers.

In the field of energy use, technicians might work to improve efficiency in industrial engineering and production line equipment. They also maintain equipment and buildings for hospitals, schools, and multifamily housing.

Technicians working in energy conservation typically work for manufacturing companies, consulting engineers, energy-audit firms, and energy-audit departments of public utility companies. They are also hired by municipal governments, hotels, architects, private builders, and manufacturers of heating, ventilating, and air-conditioning equipment. Working on a team led by an engineer, technicians determine building specifications, modify equipment and structures, audit energy use and efficiency of machines and systems, then recommend modifications or changes to save energy.

If working for a utility company, a technician might work as part of a demand-side management (DSM) program, which helps customers reduce the amount of their electric bills. DSM programs use energy conservation technicians to visit customers' homes and interview them about household energy use, such as the type of heating system, the number of people home during the day, the furnace temperature setting, and prior heating costs.

Technicians then draw a sketch of the house, measure its perimeter, windows, and doors and record dimensions on the sketch. They inspect attics, crawl spaces, and basements and note any loose-fitting windows, uninsulated pipes, and deficient insulation. They read hot-water tank labels to find the heat-loss rating and determine the need for a tank insulation blanket, and they examine air furnace filters and heat exchangers to detect dirt or soot buildup that might affect furnace operations. After discussing problems with the customer, the technician recommends repairs and provides literature on conservation improvements and sources of loans.

Energy conservation technicians must be broadly trained and systems-oriented. They must be able to work with technologically complex machinery that may contain electric motors, heaters, lamps, electronic controls, mechanical drives and linkages, optical systems, microwave systems, pneumatic and hydraulic drives, pneumatic controls, and, in some instances, radioactive samples and counters. They know how the machines are made, how the parts fit and work together, and how to figure out what is wrong if parts are not working properly. Once technicians identify the problem, they also must know how to correct it.

Requirements

High School

Students who are interested in this field should study both algebra and geometry for at least one year. Courses in physics, chemistry, machine shop, and ecology, including laboratory work, provide a solid foundation for the postsecondary program that follows. High school courses in computer science, drafting (either mechanical or architectural), and public speaking are also very helpful.

Postsecondary Training

Postsecondary programs in energy conservation focus on the principles and applications of physics, energy conservation, energy economics, instrumentation, electronics, electromechanical systems, computers, heating systems, and air-conditioning. A typical curriculum in a technical institute, community college, or other specialized two-year program offers a first year of study in physics, chemistry, mathematics, fundamentals of energy technology, energy production systems, fundamentals of electricity and electromechanical devices, and microcomputer operations.

The second year of study includes courses in mechanical and fluid systems; electrical power and illumination systems; electronic devices; blueprint reading; energy conservation; codes and regulations; heating, ventilation, and air-conditioning; technical communications; instrumentation and controls; and energy economics and audits. Considerable time is spent in laboratories, where students gain hands-on experience by assembling, disassembling, adjusting, and operating devices, mechanisms, and integrated systems of machines and controls.

Students should note that many technical colleges, community colleges, and technical institutes provide two-year programs under the specific title of energy conservation and use technology or energy management technology. In addition, many other schools offer related programs in solar power, electric power, building maintenance, equipment maintenance, and general engineering technology.

Certification or Licensing

A certificate from the National Institute for Certification in Engineering Technologies and a degree or certificate of graduation from an accredited technical program, while not required, are valuable credentials and proof of recognized preparation for work as an energy conservation technician.

Other Requirements

Students entering this field must have a practical understanding of the physical sciences, a good aptitude for math, and the ability to communicate in writing and verbally with technical specialists as well as with people not trained in the field. Their work requires a clear and precise understanding of operational and maintenance manuals, schematic drawings, blueprints, and computational formulas. The ability to communicate clearly in scientific and engineering terms is a basic requirement.

Some positions in electrical power plants require energy conservation technicians to pass certain psychological tests to predict their behavior during crises. Security clearances, arranged by the employer, are required for employment in nuclear power plants and other workplaces designated by the government as high-security facilities.

Exploring

Students who are interested in entering the field of energy conservation should obtain all the information they can from high school or postsecondary school guidance counselors and occupational information centers. School guidance counselors often can arrange field trips to industrial, commercial, and business workplaces to discuss careers in the energy efficiency field.

The electric utility company in nearly every city will have an energy analyst or a team of energy auditors in its customer service department. Energy conservation specialists also work for large hospitals, major office buildings, hotel chains, universities, and large manufacturing plants. Consulting engineers in the energy industry can be found in most major cities. Interested students may be able to talk with these energy specialists and learn about opportunities for volunteer, part-time, or summer work.

A partial understanding of the field can be gained by enrolling in seminars offered by community colleges or equipment and material suppliers on topics such as building insulation, storm windows, heat pumps, and solar heaters. Useful experience can also be obtained by undertaking student projects in solar equipment, energy audits, or energy-efficient equipment or by working with social service agencies that train volunteers to staff weatherization projects serving low-income citizens.

Employers

Energy conservation technicians are employed in many areas where energy is used, such as power plants, research laboratories, construction firms, industrial facilities, government agencies, or companies that sell and service equipment. Technicians focused in the research and development fields may work for institutions, private industry, government, and the military. Those that are focused in the field of energy use may find employment in manufacturing facilities, consulting engineering firms, energy audit firms, and energy-audit departments of utility companies. Other employers include municipal governments, manufacturers of heating and cooling equipment, private builders, hotels, and architects.

Starting Out

Most graduates of technical programs are able to secure jobs in energy conservation before graduation by working with their schools' placement offices. The placement staff works closely with potential employers, especially those that have hired graduates in recent years. Many large companies schedule regular recruiting visits to schools before graduation.

It is also possible to enter the field of energy conservation on the basis of work experience. Industrial technicians are experienced industrial equipment mechanics, and people with a background in building or home construction, plumbing, insulation, or home heating, may enter this field with the help of intensive study to supplement the knowledge and skills they bring to the job. Extensive training in military instrumentation and systems control and maintenance is also good preparation for the prospective energy conservation technician. Former Navy technicians are particularly sought in the field of energy production.

Opportunities abound for on-the-job training in energy conservation. Part-time or summer work in hospitals, major office buildings, hotel chains, and universities may be available. Some regions have youth corps, such as the Youth Energy Corps (YEC) in New York City's South Bronx, a weatherization agency that does air sealing, replaces windows, and blows high-density cellulose insulation. The workers are all high school dropouts who alternate one week of work with one week of school for one year. YEC teaches them weatherization skills and helps them earn a General Equivalency Diploma, get a job, or both.

Some jobs in energy production, such as those in electrical power plants, can be obtained with only a high school diploma. New employees, however, are expected to successfully complete company-sponsored training courses to keep their jobs and advance to positions with more responsibility.

Graduates with associate's degrees in energy conservation and use, instrumentation, electronics, or electromechanical technology will normally enter employment at a higher level, with more responsibility and higher pay, than those with less preparation. Jobs in energy research and development almost always require an associate's degree.

Some employers, such as power companies, need technicians to perform energy audits. Such a job could involve assisting energy-use auditors and energy-application analysts while they make audits or analyses in businesses or homes. This provides new technicians with a period of orientation to learn about specific duties, after which they perform regular audits and analyses on their own.

Other employers seek energy technicians to work in engineering departments. Their diverse technical training makes them promising workers in the design and modification of products.

Advancement

Because the career is relatively new, well-established patterns of advancement have not yet emerged. Nevertheless, technicians in any of the four areas of energy conservation can advance to higher positions, such as senior technicians and supervisory positions. These advanced positions require a combination of formal education, diligent on-the-job study, and special seminars or classes (usually sponsored or paid for by the employer). Technicians can also advance by progressing to new, more challenging assignments. For example, hotels, restaurants, and retail stores hire experienced energy technicians to manage energy consumption. This often involves visits to each location to audit and examine its facilities or procedures to see where energy use can be reduced. The technician then provides training in energy-saving practices. Other experienced energy technicians may be employed as special sales and customer service representatives for producers of power, energy, special control systems, or equipment designed to improve energy efficiency.

Technicians with experience and money to invest may start their own businesses, selling energy-saving products or providing audits, weatherization services, or energy-efficient renovations.

Earnings

Earnings of energy conservation technicians vary significantly based on the amount of formal training and experience. High school graduates with little or no experience who begin as trainees will earn between $15,000 and $20,000 a year in the private sector. Those who have several years of experience can earn between $35,000 to $40,000 a year. Technicians with engineering degrees who travel may earn as much as $50,000.

Technicians with military experience and three to six years of technical experience earn between $20,000 and 35,000 annually, as do graduates of postsecondary technician programs. Energy conservation technicians with five to ten years of experience in research, engineering design, or machinery engineering and maintenance can earn up to $39,000 annually.

Government and nonprofit jobs pay less than those in the private sector. Beginning technicians in weatherization programs earn a little more than $5 an hour, or about $12,000 a year. Experienced technicians in nonprofit agencies earn $12 an hour, or about $25,000 a year.

Technicians typically receive paid vacations, group insurance benefits, and employee retirement plans. In addition, they often have the benefit of company support for all or part of their educational programs, which are necessary in order to keep up-to-date with technological changes that occur in this developing field.

Work Environment

Energy conservation technicians employed in research and development, engineering design, or product planning generally work in laboratories or engineering departments with normal daytime work schedules. Other technicians often travel to customer locations or work in their employers' plants.

Work in energy production and energy use frequently involves around-the-clock operations that require shifts. In these two areas, technicians work either indoors or outdoors at the employer's site. Such assignments require little or no travel, but the work environments may be dirty, noisy, and sometimes hot or cold. Appropriate work clothing must be worn in shop and factory settings, and safety awareness and safe working habits must be practiced at all times.

Nearly all jobs in this field require energy conservation technicians to communicate in a clear, concise manner, whether orally or in the form of laboratory notebooks, reports, or letters. Energy conservation technicians who work in a plant usually interact with only a small group of people, but those who work for utility companies may have to communicate with the public while providing technical services to their customers. Energy research and development jobs involve laboratory activities and require social interaction with engineers, scientists, and other technicians. In some cases, technicians may be considered public relations representatives, which may call for special attention to dress and overall appearance.

Job stress varies. At times, the pace is relaxed but businesslike, typically in engineering, planning, and design departments or in research and development. At other times, technicians respond to urgent calls and crisis situations involving unexpected breakdowns of equipment that must be diagnosed and corrected as soon as possible. Energy technicians must be able to maintain an orderly, systematic, and objective approach to solving problems using logic and judgment.

When technicians complete an analysis of a problem in energy use and effectiveness, they can state the results in tangible dollar costs, losses, or savings, which, by helping others, can give them a sense of satisfaction. This is a highly valuable service because it provides a basis for important decisions on using and conserving energy.

Outlook

Since energy use constitutes a major expense for industry, commerce, government, institutions, and private citizens, the demand for energy conservation technicians is likely to remain strong. In addition, concerns about the availability and cost of imported fuel and increased environmental regulations necessitate energy conservation efforts.

Deregulation in the utilities industry is beginning to create opportunities for energy-service companies. Utilities, manufacturers, and government agencies are working together to establish energy-efficiency standards. The

Consortium for Energy Efficiency, for example, is a collaborative effort, involving a group of electric and gas utilities, government energy agencies, and environmental groups, to develop programs for commercial air-conditioning equipment, clothes washers, lighting, geothermal heat pumps, and industrial motor systems. These programs will create job opportunities for technicians.

The electricity industry is in the midst of significant regulatory and institutional changes. Rather than simply providing reliable electric service at the lowest cost, the industry is expected to look for ways to most profitably provide a wide array of energy services. In the past, energy conservation programs have been dominated by people with engineering and other technical skills. These skills will remain important, but as the industry becomes more customer focused, there will be a growing need for people with marketing and financial skills. Their experience will be key in selling profitable energy programs to customers.

Utility DSM programs, which have traditionally concentrated on the residential sector, are now focusing more attention on industrial and commercial facilities. With the goal of realizing larger energy savings, lower costs, and more permanent energy-efficient changes, these programs are expanding to work with contractors, builders, retailers, distributors, and manufacturers. In addition to the financial costs of purchasing natural resources, the added reality of the physical costs of depleting these important resources continues to create a greater demand for trained energy conservation employees.

For More Information

This trade association represents employees in the entire petroleum industry. Free videos, fact sheets, and informational booklets are available to educators.

American Petroleum Institute
1220 L Street, NW
Washington, DC 20005
Tel: 202-682-8000
Web: http://www.api.org

This membership organization provides information through technical seminars, certification programs, conferences, books, and journals. Members number more than 8,000 and are in the commercial, industrial, institutional, government, energy services, and utility areas.

Association of Energy Engineers
4025 Pleasantdale Road, Suite 420
Atlanta, GA 30340
Tel: 770-447-5083
Web: http://www.aeecenter.org

This nonprofit organization funded by foundations, trusts, and government contractors accelerates the adoption of sustainable energy policies and practices in developing and transitional countries. Headquartered in the United States, it has additional offices in the United Kingdom, Thailand, the Philippines, South Africa, India, and China.

International Institute for Energy Conservation
750 First Street, NE, Suite 940
Washington, DC 20002
Tel: 202-842-3388
Web: http://www.iiec.org

Environmental Engineers

Mathematics Physics	School Subjects
Leadership/management Technical/scientific	Personal Skills
Indoors and outdoors Primarily multiple locations	Work Environment
Bachelor's degree	Minimum Education Level
$20,000 to $30,000 to $40,000	Salary Range
Recommended	Certification or Licensing
About as fast as the average	Outlook

Overview

Environmental engineers design, build, and maintain systems to control waste streams produced by municipalities or private industry. Such waste streams may be wastewater, solid waste, hazardous waste, or contaminated emissions to the atmosphere (air pollution). Environmental engineers typically are employed by the Environmental Protection Agency (EPA), by private industry, or by engineering consulting firms.

History

The job of environmental engineer—like environmental lawyer, environmental planner, environmental quality analyst, and many others—is an excellent example of a professional category that has evolved to meet the booming needs of the environmental industry. Although people have been doing work that falls into the category of environmental engineering for decades, it is only within about the last 30 years that a separate professional category has been recognized for environmental engineers.

"In the 1930s, 1940s, 1950s, even the 1960s, someone who wanted to be an environmental engineer would have been steered toward sanitary engineering, which basically deals with things like wastewater, putting sewers down," says Lee DeAngelis, regional director of the Environmental Careers Organization (ECO).

Sanitary engineering, in turn, is a form of civil engineering. "Civil engineering is engineering for municipalities," explains Mike Waxman, who heads the environmental training arm of the outreach department at the University of Wisconsin-Madison College of Engineering. "It includes things like building roads, highways, buildings. But a big part of civil engineering is dealing with the waste streams that come from cities or municipalities. Wastewater from a city's sewage treatment plants is a prime example," Mike says. This water must be treated in order to be pure enough to be used again. "Scientists work out what must be done to break down the harmful substances in the water, such as by adding bacteria; engineers design, build, and maintain the systems needed to carry this out. Technicians monitor the systems, take samples, run tests, and otherwise ensure that the system is working as it should."

This structure—scientists deciding what should be done at the molecular or biological level, engineers designing the systems needed to carry out the project, and technicians taking care of the day-to-day monitoring of the systems—is applied to other waste streams as well, Mike adds.

Environmental engineering, then, is an offshoot of civil engineering/sanitary engineering and focuses on the development of the physical systems needed to control waste streams. Civil engineers who already were doing this type of work began to refer to themselves as environmental engineers around 1970, with the great boom in new environmental regulations, according to Mike. "It's what they wanted to be called," he says. "They wanted the recognition for what they were doing."

The Job

Let's say there's a small pond in Crawford County, Illinois. Normally, several different kinds of fish swim lazily through its waters, frogs hop around its banks, and birds build their nests in nearby trees. About half a mile away is the Jack J. Ryan and Sons Manufacturing Company. For years, this plant has safely treated its wastewater—the effluent produced during the manufacturing process—and discharged it into the pond. Then one day, without warning, hundreds of dead fish wash up on the banks of the pond. What's going on? What should be done? What you would do as an environmental engineer depends on several factors, including your employer and the area in which you specialize.

If you worked for the federal or state Environmental Protection Agency (EPA), your role as an environmental engineer would be like that of a police officer or detective. Your knowledge of systems to treat waste streams—coupled with your authority to enforce environmental regulations and your intimate knowledge of your territory—would make you well qualified to get to the bottom of problems stemming from systems that aren't functioning properly.

How would you tackle the Crawford County pond problem? Let's say you work in the Champaign regional office of the Illinois Environmental Protection Agency (IEPA). There are three divisions—air, land, and water—and you work in water. Your territory includes Crawford County. Alerted to the fish kill at the pond, you get into one of the state vehicles parked outside your office and head out to the site to investigate.

Once there, you snap pictures, take samples of the water, make notes. You're documenting the problem, but you're also asking yourself questions based on your knowledge of the area: Is it a discharge problem from Jack J. Ryan and Sons? If so, was there an upset in the process? A spill? A flood? Could a storage tank be leaking? Or is the problem further upstream? You know the pond is connected to other waterways; could some other discharger be responsible for killing the fish?

You'd probably pay a visit to Jack J. Ryan and Sons next. You'd talk to people there, such as the production manager. You might ask him if they have been doing anything differently lately. You also might look at plans of the plant. If the mystery remains, you might look further upstream, checking to see if other manufacturers or other wastewater dischargers are doing something new that's caused the fish kill.

When you locate the problem, the next step is enforcement. Let's say the production manager at Jack J. Ryan and Sons tells you yes, they've changed something in the manufacturing process. They're producing a new kind of die-cast part. They're sorry; they didn't know they were doing something wrong. They'll get on the problem right away.

At this point, sensing cooperation, you back off. You tell them they'll be fined $10,000, and you'll be checking back with them soon to see what they've done. But you won't turn the case over to the lawyers—yet.

Let's say that instead of working for the EPA, you're on the other side of the problem: you work for Jack J. Ryan and Sons' environmental staff. Your job is to help get the company into compliance and keep it that way, all the while balancing the economic concerns of your employer. (At one time, industries' environmental affairs positions may have been filled by workers from the plant. Since the late 1980s, however, they tend to be staffed by people dedicated strictly to environmental matters, including scientists, engineers, lawyers, and communications professionals.) One day, you get a call from an engineer at the IEPA: "There seems to be a fish kill at the pond near your plant. We've determined it's probably from a discharge from your plant." At this point, you'd jump up and get busy. You'd probably look at your plant's plans, talk to the production manager, and figure out a plan of action. If you were having trouble coming up with a plan, you might turn to a consulting engineering firm for help.

As an environmental engineer with a consulting firm, you'd apply your expertise to problems your firm's clients were having. If Jack J. Ryan and Sons called your company for help, for example, you might be part of a team that goes out to the plant, assesses the problem, and designs a system to get the plant back into compliance. Consulting firms balance what the client wants, needs, and can afford. They know the technical aspects of waste control and also may sell clients on their expertise in dealing with the government—filling out the required government forms, for example.

Broadly speaking, environmental engineers may focus on one of three areas: *air, land,* or *water.* Air includes air pollution control, air quality management, and other specialties involved in dealing with systems to treat emissions. The private sector tends to have the majority of these jobs, according to ECO. Land includes landfill professionals, for whom environmental engineering and public health are key areas. Water includes activities like those described above.

A big area for environmental engineers is hazardous waste management. Expertise in designing systems and processes to reduce, recycle, and treat hazardous waste streams is very much in demand, according to ECO. This area tends to be the most technical of all the environmental fields and so demands more professionals with graduate and technical degrees.

Environmental engineers spend a lot of time on paperwork—including writing reports and memos and filling out forms. They also might climb a smokestack, wade in a creek, or go toe-to-toe with a district attorney in a battle over a compliance matter. If they work on in-house staffs, they may face frustration over not knowing what is going on in their own plants. If they work for the government, they might struggle with bureaucracy. If they work for a consultant, they may have to juggle the needs of the client (including the need to keep costs down) with the demands of the government.

Requirements

High School

A bachelor's degree is mandatory to work in environmental engineering. At the high school level, the most important course work is in science and mathematics. It's also good to develop written communication skills. Competition to get into the top engineering schools is tough, so make sure you do well on your ACT or SAT tests.

Postsecondary Training

At this writing, about 20 schools offer an undergraduate degree in environmental engineering. Other possibilities are to earn a civil engineering, mechanical engineering, industrial engineering, or other traditional engineering degree with an environmental focus; to obtain a traditional engineering degree and pick up the environmental knowledge on the job; or to obtain a masters' degree in environmental engineering.

Certification or Licensing

If your work as an engineer affects public health, safety, or property, you must register with the state. To obtain registration, you must have a degree from an accredited engineering program. Right before you get your degree (or soon after), you must pass an engineer-in-training (EIT) exam covering fundamentals of science and engineering. A few years after you've started your career, you also must pass an exam covering engineering practice. Additional certification is voluntary and may be obtained through such organizations as the American Academy of Environmental Engineers.

Other Requirements

People who like solving problems, have a good background in science and math—who could draw on their knowledge of differential equations if they had to, for example—and could, in the words of one engineer, "just get in there and figure out what needs to be done," are good candidates for this position.

Exploring

A good way to explore becoming an environmental engineer is to talk to someone in the field. Contact your local EPA office, check the Yellow Pages for environmental consulting firms in your area, or ask a local industrial company if you can visit. The latter is not as far-fetched as you might think: big industry has learned the value of earning positive community relations, and their outreach efforts may include having an open house for their neighbors in which one can walk through their plants, ask questions, and get a feel for what goes on there.

You cannot practice at being an environmental engineer without having a bachelor's degree. However, you can put yourself in situations in which you're around environmental engineers to see what they do and how they work. To do so, you may volunteer for the local chapter of a nonprofit environmental organization, do an internship through ECO or another organization, or work first as an environmental technician, a job that requires less education (such as a two-year associate's degree or even a high school diploma).

Another good way to get a feel for a field is to familiarize yourself with its professional journals. Two journals that may be available in your library include *Chemical & Engineering News,* which regularly features articles on waste management systems, and *Pollution Engineering,* which features articles of interest to environmental engineers.

Employers

Environmental engineers most often work for the Environmental Protection Agency (EPA), in private industry, or at engineering consulting firms.

Starting Out

The traditional method of entering this field is by obtaining a bachelor's degree and applying directly to companies or to the EPA. School placement offices can assist you in these efforts.

Advancement

After you've worked for a time as an environmental engineer, there are several routes for advancement. If you start out with the EPA, you may become a department supervisor or switch to private industry or consulting. In-house environmental staff members may rise to supervisory positions. Engineers with consulting firms may become project managers or specialists in certain areas.

Environmental careers are evolving at a breakneck speed. New specialties are emerging all the time. Your advancement may take the form of getting in on—maybe even helping to develop—some subspecialty yet to be invented that suits your own particular interests, experience, and expertise.

Earnings

The following salary information is from ECO:

Average solid waste management pay is slightly lower than that for hazardous waste management. Entry-level salaries for professionals in this field range from less than $20,000 to $30,000, with engineers at the higher end of the scale. In water quality management, the range is about $30,000 to $40,000 for state and federal government jobs and $30,000 and up for private jobs.

Fringe benefits vary widely depending on the employer. State EPA jobs may include, for example, two weeks of vacation, health insurance, tuition reimbursement, use of company vehicles for work, and similar perks. In-house or consulting positions may add additional benefits in order to lure top candidates.

Work Environment

You're likely to split your time between working in an office and working out in the field (or, if you're a member of an in-house staff, out in your plant or at the site of discharges). You also may go to court. Since ongoing education is crucial in most of these positions, you'll spend time in school, at workshops, and studying up on new regulations, techniques, and problems. It's important to be able to work as part of a team that may include any of a number of different specialists. It's also important to be able to communicate well, both in writing and in discussions. You must be comfortable with technical information, be able to apply your background in math and science, and preferably be able to communicate often-complex engineering information to people who may not have the type of technical background that you do.

Outlook

The 1980s were a time of increased environmental regulation and enforcement. Superfund legislation forced states to clean up hazardous waste sites and the U.S. Environmental Protection Agency required companies to reduce waste and dispose of it more responsibly. Environmental engineers, consequently, had abundant opportunities. In the 1990s, many of the major cleanup efforts were undertaken or finished, causing the environmental engineering job market to taper off from its rapid growth.

The Clean Air Act of 1990 did create a brief surge in air pollution jobs. Overall, however, the water supply and water pollution control specialties presently offer the most job opportunities for environmental engineers.

Opportunities are available with all three major employers—the EPA, industry, and consulting firms. The EPA has long been a big employer of environmental engineers. At this writing, private industry and consultants are hiring more and more of them.

For More Information

For information on certification, careers, and salaries or a copy of Environmental Engineering Selection Guide *(giving names of accredited environmental engineering programs and of professors who have board certification as environmental engineers), contact:*

American Academy of Environmental Engineers
130 Holiday Court, Suite 100
Annapolis, MD 21401
Tel: 410-266-3311
Web: http://www.enviro-engrs.org

For guidance information or a videotape explaining many types of engineering ($20), contact:

Junior Engineering Technical Society, Inc.
1420 King Street, Suite 405
Alexandria, VA 22314-2794
Tel: 703-548-5387
Email: jets@nae.edu
Web: http://www.asee.org/external/jets/default.html

A cross-disciplinary environmental association:

National Association of Environmental Professionals
6524 Ramoth Drive
Jacksonville, FL 32226-3202
Tel: 904-251-9900
Web: http://www.naep.org

National Solid Wastes Management Association
4301 Connecticut Avenue, NW, Suite 300
Washington, DC 20008
Tel: 202-244-4700
Web: http://www.envasns.org/nswma

Environmental Lobbyists

English Government Speech	School Subjects
Communication/ideas Helping/teaching Leadership/management	Personal Skills
Primarily indoors Primarily multiple locations	Work Environment
Bachelor's degree	Minimum Education Level
$12,000 to $40,000 to $80,000	Salary Range
None available	Certification or Licensing
About as fast as the average	Outlook

Overview

Lobbyists are people who strive to influence legislation on behalf of a special interest group or a client. Like other lobbyists, *environmental lobbyists* strive to influence state or federal legislation in order to achieve a goal or to benefit a special interest group. Environmental lobbyists, however, deal specifically with environmental issues. They urge legislators and other government officials to support measures to protect endangered species, limit the exploitation of natural resources, and impose stricter antipollution regulations.

History

Occasionally looked upon as mere influence peddlers, lobbyists actually serve an important role in the democratic process. Government officials and legislators must understand and make decisions about innumerable issues.

They cannot possibly be experts in every area. Consequently, many rely upon lobbyists to provide them with information about important issues. Environmental lobbyists compile information about the probable impact of various measures on the environment and are sometimes invited by legislators to help them draft new bills.

The Job

Environmental lobbyists strive to influence legislators and government officials through both direct and indirect lobbying. Direct lobbying involves reaching legislators themselves. Environmental lobbyists meet with members of Congress, their staff members, and other members of government. They call government officials to discuss the impact various measures might have on the environment. They sometimes testify before congressional committees or state legislatures. They distribute letters and fact sheets to legislators' offices. They sometimes try to approach legislators as they travel to and from their offices, and some lobbyists ask legislators who share their views to broach issues with other, less sympathetic legislators.

In another form of direct lobbying, environmental lobbyists strive to persuade members of Congress to serve as cosponsors for bills the lobbyists support. When a member of Congress becomes a cosponsor of a bill, his or her name is added to the list of members supporting that measure. Lobbyists typically assume that cosponsors will vote to support the bill. They also use the list of cosponsors to influence other members of Congress to support a measure. A bill's chances of one day becoming a law dramatically improve as more members agree to serve as cosponsors.

Indirect lobbying, also called grassroots lobbying, involves educating and motivating the public. The goal of indirect lobbying is to encourage members of the public to urge their representatives to vote for or against certain legislation. Environmental lobbyists use an array of indirect techniques. They issue press releases about pending legislation, hoping to inspire members of the media to write topical articles. They mail letters to citizens, urging them to write or call their representatives. They post information on the Internet and sometimes go door-to-door with information to mobilize members of environmental groups. On rare occasions, they take concerned citizens to state capitals or to Washington, DC, to meet with representatives.

For both direct and indirect lobbying efforts, environmental lobbyists try to form coalitions with other environmental groups. Members of these coalitions work together because they have a common interest in protecting the environment. By pooling information and resources, members of the coalition can be more effective in reaching the public and members of government.

Some environmental lobbyists also support political candidates who are likely to support measures that protect the environment. They promote these candidates by distributing positive information to the public and by raising money for their campaigns.

Requirements

No one academic path leads directly to a lobbying career. Most lobbyists come to the profession from other disciplines and other jobs. Some have political experience, others have scientific, economic, or legal backgrounds. This previous experience can be extremely useful to environmental lobbyists because they must be able to assess the environmental and economic impact and to identify the legal strengths or weaknesses of various measures.

High School

The best way to prepare yourself for this field is by pursuing a well-rounded education. You should, of course, study civics and history to gain an understanding of our country's political system. You also should take biology, ecology, and chemistry in order to learn about the scientific issues behind environmental legislation.

In addition to understanding politics and science, lobbyists must have a number of very practical skills, including the ability to use computers and the ability to write and speak clearly. You should, therefore, take computer courses, speech classes, and English.

Postsecondary Training

While there are no specific requirements for environmental lobbyists, most have college degrees; a growing number also have advanced degrees.

During your undergraduate studies, you should continue to take courses that will help you understand the complex issues behind legislation and gain the practical skills that will make you an effective lobbyist. You should take courses in environmental science, geography, and geology. You should also study political science and history, which will help you understand how our political system developed and help you prepare to function within that system. Finally, study economics, because lobbyists must be able to assess the probable economic impact of pending legislation.

Lobbyists must be able to do more than understand the issues, however—they must also be able to write and speak about them. They must be able to influence the way other people think about issues. Communication, public relations, and English all can be helpful courses for the future environmental lobbyist.

Students who choose to pursue advanced degrees will find that having special areas of expertise, such as ecology, economics, or law, coupled with broad undergraduate backgrounds, will help them find interesting positions.

Consider serving as an intern for environmental organizations. Some colleges and universities will award academic credits for internship experiences. Internships can also help you gain hands-on experience, learn about the issues, and meet potential employers. Serving as interns, says Cindy Shogan, an environmental lobbyist for the Southern Utah Wilderness Alliance, "can help students decide what they want to do within the environmental movement. It gives them a better idea of the options. It also helps them learn about other environmental organizations, so they can decide which ones appeal most to them philosophically."

Political or government experience is also invaluable for would-be lobbyists. Try to land a staff position within a legislator's offices or pursue government internships. Several agencies in Washington, DC, offer government internships. Among these are the Library of Congress, the U.S. Department of Agriculture, and the School of International Service at American University.

Certification or Licensing

Although there is no certification process for lobbyists, federal law does require lobbyists to register if they lobby among federal agencies or bodies. Many states also regulate lobbyists' activities. Some require lobbyists to file reports outlining their activities. For additional information about the registration requirements for lobbyists, contact your state government or the American League of Lobbyists.

Other Requirements

Environmental lobbyists must be tenacious, self-motivated individuals. They must have excellent communications skills. They must be able to work well in teams and perform well under pressure. They must understand the political process. Because lobbyists must be able to approach government officials and powerful legislators, they should be confident, outgoing individuals. Most important, environmental lobbyists must be committed to protecting the environment.

"Environmental lobbyists," says Cindy, "have to be able to think quickly on their feet. If one approach isn't working, they have to be able to shift gears. They have to be flexible. They also have to have a keen strategic sense. They have to be able to look at all the angles and really think through a course of action."

According to Kevin Kirchner, an environmental lobbyist for Earthjustice Legal Defense Fund, a sense of humor can be a vital tool for an environmental lobbyist. "This is high stress work," he explains. "It's easy to get frustrated. You've got to be able to find humor in what's going on. I also think environmental lobbyists must have an unwavering dedication to accuracy and the truth. Legislators will only listen to lobbyists who have credibility."

Exploring

You can gain valuable practical experience by volunteering with an environmental organization. This practical experience can help you understand the issues and obstacles that environmental lobbyists encounter. By volunteering to work for local political campaigns or by serving as a page in Congress, you can learn about our country's political system. If you really feel this career might be for you, try landing an internship with an environmental organization or government agency.

Employers

Many of our country's most respected environmental protection organizations employ environmental lobbyists. The Nature Conservancy, Sierra Club, National Wildlife Federation, Wilderness Society, and Friends of the Earth are just a few of the organizations that are actively involved in lobbying on behalf of our environment.

Starting Out

Students interested in becoming environmental lobbyists should contact various environmental organizations to discuss lobbying activities.

Advancement

Environmental lobbyists can advance by gaining experience, demonstrating their abilities, or earning advanced degrees. In large environmental organizations, they also may encounter opportunities to assume management responsibilities.

Unlike lobbyists who work for special interest groups that represent major industries, environmental lobbyists are rarely motivated by ambition. Most choose the profession out of a genuine desire to protect our country's natural resources.

Earnings

Environmental lobbyists usually work for not-for-profit organizations with extremely limited budgets. Consequently, their salaries tend to be much lower than those of other lobbyists. While most lobbyists may earn anywhere from $12,000 to $700,000, depending on the groups they represent and their years of experience, environmental lobbyists are more likely to earn between $12,000 and $80,000.

"I would be shocked," says Cindy, "to learn that any of my colleagues were earning more than $80,000."

Kevin comments, "Environmental lobbyists must have an enormous commitment on a personal level because they just don't get paid as much as they could in other jobs and they often work longer hours."

Work Environment

Because most environmental lobbyists work for not-for-profit organizations, they often have limited staff and even more limited budgets. Consequently, environmental lobbyists usually combine highly professional skills, such as scientific or legal expertise, with clerical capabilities. In other words, environmental lobbyists must be willing to stuff envelopes as well as meet with senators.

According to Cindy, lobbyists' schedules are determined by Congress's schedule. "If Congress is on break," she says, "people dress more casually and spend time catching up on research, paperwork, and grassroots lobbying. When Congress is in session, you're in constant crisis mode." Crisis mode for an environmental lobbyist entails 12- and 14-hour days, irregular hours, and frequent trips to Capitol Hill.

Environmental lobbyists often face frustrating setbacks. Measures they support can take years to wend their way through Congress. Along the way, they can be altered and weakened almost beyond recognition. This can be stressful and disappointing, but environmental lobbyists must be able to put these feelings aside and move on to the next challenge.

Outlook

Regrettably, there is no shortage of environmental concerns in our country. As long as people continue to pollute our air and water, cut down forests, develop land, and mine the earth, environmental groups will continue to fight for legislation that will protect our natural resources. This profession is, therefore, expected to grow about as fast as the average through 2006.

The nation's economy can affect environmental protection organizations, which are largely funded by donations. During recessions, people may not be able to give as generously to not-for-profit organizations. Environmental protection organizations may, in turn, be forced to cut back on their lobbying efforts.

For More Information

For career information, contact:

American League of Lobbyists
PO Box 30005
Alexandria, VA 22310
Tel: 703-960-3011
Email: info@alldc.org
Web: http://www.alldc.org/

ECO provides career information, publications, and internship information, among many other services.

Environmental Careers Organization
179 South Street
Boston, MA 02111
Tel: 617-426-4375
Web: http://www.eco.org/

Foresters

Earth science English Mathematics	School Subjects
Helping/teaching Leadership/management Technical/scientific	Personal Skills
Indoors and outdoors Primarily one location	Work Environment
Bachelor's degree	Minimum Education Level
$19,500 to $35,800 to $75,000	Salary Range
None available	Certification or Licensing
About as fast as the average	Outlook

Overview

Foresters protect and manage forest resources, one of our greatest natural assets, through various biological techniques. Using their specialized knowledge of tree biology and ecology, wood science, and manufacturing processes, they manage forests for timber production, protect them from fire and pest damage, harvest mature forests, and re-establish new forests after harvesting mature ones.

There are more than 37,000 foresters working in the United States today. More than half are employed by federal, state, and local government agencies. While there are foresters' positions in every state, the majority of them are concentrated in the Western and Southeastern states.

History

Not so long ago, forests were considered a hindrance to farming, a barrier to settlement, and a surplus commodity of minimal value to a small population of settlers. No profession existed to protect and manage the forests. As the U.S. population grew and land clearing increased in the mid-19th century, however, people with foresight realized that forests were becoming more valuable and, unless protected, might disappear entirely. Laws enacted by the federal and state governments around that time helped to slow down forest destruction. At the same time, opening the Western territories to farming allowed forests to reclaim marginal farms abandoned in the East.

In 1900, seven individuals founded the Society of American Foresters. At that time, they embodied practically the whole profession of forestry. By 1905, the U.S. Forest Service was established within the Department of Agriculture. Two years later, the Forest Service assumed responsibility for managing the newly established national forests.

Today, there are 156 national forests staffed by professional foresters. There are also many forest lands owned by states and municipalities. The largest segment of the forest land, however, is in private ownership, with individuals and corporations owning 72 percent of all U.S. forests. In all, forests still cover almost one-third of the nation. Because of the growing awareness that forest resources need to be managed wisely, the forestry profession has developed rapidly. Foresters and forestry technicians are charged with protecting the nation's forests from fire, insects, and diseases; managing them for wood crops, water, wildlife, and forage; preserving their beauty and making it accessible; and training others to carry on their work.

The Job

Foresters do much of their work outdoors, especially during the early part of their careers. Ralph Unversaw, a district forester for Indiana, still spends most of his time outdoors. "Normally, I spend about four days out of a five-day workweek outside, and the fifth inside trying to catch up on paperwork," he says. Most of Ralph's job involves working with private woodland owners to manage their properties. "My job is to promote forest management," he says. "If they want to do some sort of timber management, I can advise them on planting, selecting trees for harvest, and harvesting."

Beginning foresters perform many duties. They may map areas of a forest and estimate the amounts of resources, such as timber, game shelter, and food, water, and forage for cattle and sheep, that they provide. They may also determine areas that need intervention, such as planting trees, scattering seed from helicopters, controlling disease or insects, thinning dense forest stands, or pruning trees to produce better lumber or plywood. They may monitor stands of trees to ensure healthy growth and determine the best time for harvesting. They may lay out logging roads or roads to lakes and recreational facilities and create the plans for building wilderness areas. Foresters may supervise crews doing all these jobs and inspect their work after it is done.

Foresters select and mark trees to be cut and check on the cutting and removal of the logs and pulpwood. They may be in charge of the lookouts, patrols, and pilots who detect fires and may lead crews that fight fires. They also sometimes oversee the operation of recreational areas, collect fees, issue permits, give talks to groups of campers, find lost hikers, and rescue climbers and skiers.

Even for foresters in the early stages of their careers, however, the work is not all outdoors. They must record the work done in the forest on maps and in reports. They use computers, data-processing equipment, and aerial photography to assist in this process. Although most beginning foresters do most of their work outside, some do work primarily indoors, in the technical laboratories and factories of wood-using industries. They may work in sawmills, plywood and hardboard plants, pulp and paper mills, wood preserving plants, and furniture factories. These foresters are specialists in wood technology or pulp and paper technology. Many forest scientists work in laboratories and greenhouses, as well as in the forests, to learn how trees and forests grow.

When used wisely, a forest offers many benefits and can be used for several purposes. To maximize these benefits and purposes, foresters must not only know a great deal about the forest resources, but also be able to understand people, explain technical information to them, and secure their cooperation. Foresters, from the very start of their careers, can expect to be called on to speak before various groups, from elementary school classes to service clubs and meetings of scientific societies. While not all foresters are in frequent contact with the public, they all eventually discover that their advancement depends on their ability to work with other people. "In my job, I have to do a lot of public relations-type work," says Ralph. "I provide a lot of educational programs to the public—both to youth and to adults."

Much of the work that foresters do involves the application of scientific knowledge and theory to actual practice in the field. Some foresters specialize in one or two of the basic sciences. In fact, some foresters are engaged in research that delves deeply into the fundamental physical and biological sciences. They work in laboratories with many modern techniques and devices.

The scientific knowledge of how forests live is the specialty of *silvicul-turists,* who practice the art of establishing or reproducing forests, regulating their makeup, and influencing their growth and development along prede-termined lines. The art of silviculture and the principles of economics and finance are the foundations of forest preservation and management.

One branch of forestry, known as forest engineering or logging engi-neering, straddles the border between forestry and engineering. Work in this field includes the design and construction of roads, bridges, dams, and buildings in forest areas. The design, selection, and installation of equipment for moving logs and pulpwood out of the forest is the special field of the *log-ging,* or *forest, engineer.* Forest and logging engineers may be graduates of schools of forestry that offer courses in this specialty, or they may have been trained as civil, mechanical, or electrical engineers.

Another type of specialist, the *forest ecologist,* conducts research to find out how forests are affected by changes in environmental conditions, such as soil, light, climate, altitude, and animal populations.

Foresters use a number of tools to perform their jobs: clinometers mea-sure the heights, diameter tapes measure the diameters, and increment bor-ers and bark gauges measure the growth of trees. Photogrammetry and remote sensing (aerial photographs taken from airplanes and satellites) are often used for mapping large forest areas and detecting widespread trends of forest and land use. Computers are used extensively, both in the office and in the field, for the storage, retrieval, and analysis of the information required to manage the forest land and its resources.

In most forestry organizations and groups, a great deal of physical work in the woods needs to be done. This work is usually done by people with experience and aptitude but little formal education beyond high school or by forest technicians who have graduated from one- or two-year programs in forest technicians' institutes or ranger schools.

Requirements

In preparation for becoming a forester, Ralph obtained a bachelor's degree in forestry and wildlife management. The minimal educational requirement to enter this career is a bachelor's degree in forestry; however, some foresters combine three years of liberal arts education with two years of professional education in forestry and receive the degrees of bachelor of arts and master of forestry. There are approximately 48 schools of forestry in the United States with programs accredited by the Society of American Foresters, the professional society to which most foresters belong. Schools of forestry are found in 38 states, most of them associated with state universities.

High School

To prepare for entry into a college forestry program, you will need to specifically focus on English and mathematics. Mastery of these subjects will help you gain admission to and have success at a good school. Forestry students must read widely, rapidly, and with understanding and be able to speak well. History, languages, chemistry, and physics are also important.

Postsecondary Training

The courses of study in all accredited schools of forestry have the same fundamental components. To be accredited, a school must offer a specified amount of instruction in four essential areas of study: *forest management* (the application of business methods and silvicultural principles to the operation of forest properties), *forest ecology and biology* (ecosystem management and physiological principles including fires, insects, diseases, wildlife, and weather), *forest policy and administration* (understanding legislative procedures and environmental regulations that influence management decisions), and *forest measurements* (the inventory process for quantifying forest resources such as timber amount and quality, wildlife habitat, water quality, and recreational potential). The courses in these four topics, which are generally concentrated in the junior and senior years, make up the professional portion of the forester's schooling.

To prepare for these subjects, forestry students need a grounding in mathematics, surveying, chemistry, physics, botany, zoology, soil science, economics, and geology. Moreover, to help develop the skills needed for self-education later in their careers, students take basic courses in literature, social studies, and writing. All these courses are organized in a program that fills the freshman and sophomore years largely with basic sciences and humanities.

Foresters also do fieldwork as a part of their university training. Some schools of forestry are so close to forests that regular three-hour or all-day laboratory sessions are conducted in the school forest. Following the sophomore year in many schools of forestry is a summer camp period of 8 to 11 weeks. This is basically a continuous laboratory period during which the students take part in the life of the forest, and under guidance of the faculty, store up experience on which they will draw in their junior and senior professional courses. In addition, some schools of forestry require that their students spend an entire summer working for a forestry organization such as the U.S. Forest Service, National Park Service, a state forest service, or a company in the forest industry. The employer usually reports back to the school on the student's progress.

In addition to the basic sciences and humanities and the four core forestry areas of study, elective courses are offered to enable students to specialize in such fields as forest or logging engineering, wood technology, range management, wildlife management, forest recreation, and watershed management.

Graduates of forestry schools who wish to specialize in a certain area or broaden their general knowledge of forestry or related fields may opt for graduate work at one of the forestry schools to earn master's degrees or doctorates.

Other Requirements

Forestry requires above-average intelligence. Because of the nature of the work, the forester must often make decisions on the basis of incomplete knowledge. This means that the individual in this field must be self-reliant and have a high degree of initiative. A forester should have an aptitude for science, natural curiosity, and a strong liking for the outdoors. Because trees grow slowly and the changes in forests are gradual, foresters must have greater-than-average patience and a firm conviction that the work they do is important. If one makes mistakes or is careless, the results may not be apparent for many years. Therefore, the forester must be dependable and conscientious. While it is not necessary for foresters to have the physical attributes of athletes, they must have greater-than-average endurance and should enjoy physical activity.

Exploring

One way to explore the field of forestry is to talk with someone already working as a forester or forestry technician. In some parts of the country, local chapters of the Society of American Foresters invite prospective forestry students to some of their meetings and field trips. School guidance counselors may have literature and information on forestry careers. Also, colleges and universities that offer forestry degrees should have information packets for interested students.

If you live near forested areas you might be able to find summer or part-time jobs in forestry. Unskilled workers are sometimes used for certain tasks, and this type of work could be a good introduction to the field by providing valuable experience and offering a view of what the job of a forester is really like.

Employers

Federal, state, and local governments are by far the largest employers of foresters. According to the U.S. Bureau of Labor Statistics, foresters and conservation scientists held approximately 37,000 jobs in the late 1990s. Of those, almost 30 percent of all salaried employees worked for the federal government, mostly in the United States Department of Agriculture's (USDA) Forest Service. Another 30 percent were employed by state governments, and 10 percent worked for local governments.

The remaining foresters work in private industry or are self-employed as consulting foresters. For those who work in private industry, employers include logging and lumber companies, sawmills, and research and testing facilities. Consulting foresters usually work with private or corporate owners of woodlands to help them manage their forests in the best way posssible.

There are foresters employed in every state. The largest number of foresters' jobs, however, are in the Western and Southeastern states, where there are many national and private forests, as well as commercial ones.

Starting Out

According to Ralph, it is not easy to find a forester's position. "I was fairly lucky because there happened to be a job opening right when I applied," he says. "There just aren't that many foresters' jobs and the competition is tough."

Because the majority of foresters are employed by government agencies, forestry school graduates might first pursue this avenue of employment. Job seekers should check with their state and local governments for job listings, as well as with federal agencies, such as the Forest Service, Bureau of Land Management, National Park Service, and Bureau of Indian Affairs. Beginning foresters are often hired for government jobs on the basis of competitive civil service examinations.

Other foresters work for private industry, primarily for companies that manage forest lands for lumber, pulpwood, and other products. Newly graduated foresters should check with their college placement offices for information on job opportunities. Reference sections of local libraries may contain directories of wood products manufacturers, pulp and paper mills, timber firms, and conservation groups, all of which may employ foresters. Finally, the Society of American Foresters maintains a listing of resources for the forestry job seeker.

Advancement

Professional foresters who have graduated from university-level schools of forestry often begin at their first job with work that is not at a fully professional level. They may, for example, do the elementary surveying involved in forest inventory or engineering projects, work in logging or construction crews, or act as supervisors of planting or insect control crews. In progressive organizations, this training period is kept short and is meant to provide a real understanding of operations from the bottom up.

After such a training period, foresters are usually moved to more responsible positions. This almost always means an increase in office work and a corresponding decrease in the time spent in physical work in the field.

As foresters move on to positions of greater responsibility in a public or private forestry organization, they may be placed in a line position. A line position is one in which the forester supervises technicians and other foresters. At the lower levels, the forester in a line position might directly supervise two to five other foresters; at higher levels the forester may still oversee only a small number of people, but with each of them, in turn, being in charge of a small group of foresters. Success in a line position requires not only professional competence and knowledge but also the sort of personality that makes a leader.

Other foresters may move into research. In research work, the forester may begin as a laboratory assistant, work gradually into detailed research activities, and eventually move into leadership or administrative positions in forestry research. Some foresters who move into research choose to return to school for further education. With an advanced degree, such as a master's or doctorate, comes more opportunity for advancement, as well as better pay.

Earnings

Foresters with bachelor's degrees who are employed by the federal government earn average starting salaries of $19,500 to $24,000, depending on their college records. Those with master's degrees can earn starting salaries of between $24,200 and $29,600, while those with doctorates start at around $35,800, or in research positions, $42,900. Experienced foresters may eventually make up to $75,000. Foresters working for the federal government in nonsupervisory, supervisory, and managerial positions earn an average salary of approximately $47,500.

Starting salaries for foresters in private industry are comparable to starting salaries in the federal government, but starting salaries in state and local governments are generally somewhat lower. Whether working for private industry or federal, state, or local governments, foresters' salaries depend on the number of years of education and their experience in the field. Workers in this industry usually receive a benefits package that includes health insurance, paid vacations, and sick leave.

Work Environment

Foresters generally work a 40-hour week, although they must be prepared for overtime duty, particularly when emergency conditions arise. In the field, foresters encounter many different conditions, such as snow, rain, freezing cold, or extreme heat. They may sometimes be faced with hazardous conditions, such as forest fires.

The day-to-day duties of a forester in the field are often strenuous. "The job can be physically demanding," Ralph says. "There's often a lot of walking."

Foresters whose work is more research-centered may not find the physical requirements as demanding since they may be spending more time in the laboratory. Their work week also tends to be more regular and their routines somewhat less varied.

Most who choose a career in this field love nature and the outdoors; for them, a great benefit is being able to work in a beautiful, natural setting, free from the confines of a desk job in an office. "It's a great job if you like to be outdoors and walk through the woods," Ralph says. "That's what I like best about it."

Outlook

According to the U.S. Bureau of Labor Statistics, employment of foresters is expected to increase about as fast as the average for all occupations through the year 2006. Budgetary limitations have led to cutbacks in federal programs, where employment is concentrated. Prospects for foresters outside the federal government are expected to be better, however. Demand at the state and local levels should continue to increase due to emphasis on environmental protection and responsible land management. Some growth is also expected in private industry, which may need additional personnel to improve logging and milling practices in order to reduce waste.

For More Information

For information on forestry and forests in the United States, contact:

American Forests
PO Box 2000
Washington, DC 20013
Tel: 202-955-4500
Email: acf@igc.apc.org
Web: http://www.amfor.org

For information on forestry careers, schools, and job opportunities in the United States, contact:

Society of American Foresters
5400 Grosvenor Lane
Bethesda, MD 20814-2198
Tel: 301-897-8720
Email: safweb@safnet.org
Web: http://www.safnet.org

For information about government careers in forestry, contact:

USDA Forest Service
2nd Floor, Central Wing
PO Box 96090
Washington, DC 20090-6090
Tel: 202-205-8333
Web: http://www.fs.fed.us

For information on forestry careers in Canada, contact:

Canadian Forestry Association
185 Somerset Street West, Suite 203
Ottawa, ON K2P 0J2 Canada
Tel: 613-232-1815
Email: cfa@cyberus.ca

Geologists

School Subjects	Earth science Geography
Personal Skills	Helping/teaching Technical/scientific
Work Environment	Indoors and outdoors One location with some travel
Minimum Education Level	Bachelor's degree
Salary Range	$30,900 to $48,400 to $59,700
Certification or Licensing	None available
Outlook	About as fast as the average

Overview

Geologists study all aspects of the earth, including its origin, history, composition, and structure. Along more practical lines, geologists may, through the use of theoretical knowledge and research data, locate groundwater, oil, minerals, and other natural resources. They play an increasingly important role in studying, preserving, and cleaning up the environment. They advise construction companies and government agencies on the suitability of locations being considered for buildings, highways, and other structures. They also prepare geological reports, maps, and diagrams.

History

Geology is a young science first developed by early mining engineers. In the late 18th century, scientists such as A. G. Werner and James Hutton, a retired British physician, created a sensation with their differing theories on the origins of rocks. Through the study of fossils and the development of geological maps, others continued to examine the history of the earth in the 19th century.

From these beginnings, geology has made rapid advances, both in scope and knowledge. With the development of more intricate technology, geologists are able to study areas of the earth that they were previously unable to reach. Seismographs, for example, measure energy waves resulting from the earth's movement in order to determine the location and intensity of earthquakes. Seismic prospecting involves bouncing sound waves off buried rock layers.

The Job

The geologist's work includes locating and obtaining physical data and material. This may necessitate the drilling of deep holes to obtain samples, the collection and examination of the materials found on or under the earth's surface, or the use of instruments to measure the earth's gravity and magnetic field. Some geologists may spend three to six months of each year in fieldwork. In laboratory work, geologists carry out studies based on field research. Sometimes working under controlled temperatures or pressures, geologists analyze the chemical and physical properties of geological specimens, such as rock, fossil remains, and soil. Once the data is analyzed and the studies are completed, geologists, and *geological technicians* write reports based on their research.

A wide variety of laboratory instruments are used, including X-ray diffractometers, which determine the crystal structure of minerals, and petrographic microscopes for the study of rock and sediment samples.

Geologists working to protect the environment may design and monitor waste disposal sites, preserve water supplies, and reclaim contaminated land and water to comply with more stringent federal environmental regulations.

Geologists often specialize in one of the disciplines listed below.

Marine geologists study the oceans, including the seabed and subsurface features.

Paleontologists specialize in the study of the earth's rock formations, including remains of plant and animal life, in order to understand earth's evolution and estimate its age.

Geochronologists are geoscientists who use radioactive dating and other techniques to estimate the age of rock and other samples from an exploration site.

Petroleum geologists attempt to locate natural gas and oil deposits through exploratory testing and study of the data obtained. They recommend the acquisition of new properties and the retention or release of properties already owned by their companies. They also estimate oil reserves and assist petroleum engineers in determining exact production procedures. Closely related to petroleum geologists are *economic geologists,* who search for new resources of minerals and fuels.

Engineering geologists are responsible for the application of geological knowledge to problems arising in the construction of roads, buildings, bridges, dams, and other structures.

Mineralogists are interested in the classification of minerals composing rocks and mineral deposits. To this end, they examine and analyze the physical and chemical properties of minerals and precious stones to develop data and theories on their origin, occurrence, and possible uses in industry and commerce.

Petrologists study the origin of igneous, metamorphic, and sedimentary rocks.

Stratigraphers study the distribution and relative arrangement of sedimentary rock layers. This enables them to understand evolutionary changes in fossils and plants, which leads to an understanding of successive changes in the distribution of land and sea.

Closely related to stratigraphers are *sedimentologists,* who determine processes and products involved in sedimentary rock formations.

Geohydrologists study the nature and distribution of water within the earth and are often involved in environmental impact studies.

Geomorphologists study the form of the earth's surface and the processes, such as erosion and glaciation, that bring about changes.

The geologist is far from limited in a choice of work, but a basic knowledge of all sciences is essential in each of these specializations. An increasing number of scientists combine geology with detailed knowledge in another field. *Geochemists,* for example, are concerned with the chemical composition of, and the changes in, minerals and rocks, while *planetary geologists* apply their knowledge of geology to interpret surface conditions on the moon and other planets.

Requirements

High School

High school students should study earth science, physics, computer science, geography, social studies, mathematics, and English.

Postsecondary Training

A bachelor's degree is the minimum requirement for entry into lower-level geology jobs, but a master's degree is usually necessary for beginning positions in research, teaching, or exploration. A person with a strong background in physics, chemistry, mathematics, or computer science may also qualify for some geology jobs. For those wishing to make significant advancements in research and college-level teaching, a doctoral degree is required. Those interested in the geological profession should have an aptitude not only for geology but also for physics, chemistry, and mathematics.

A number of colleges, universities, and institutions of technology offer degrees in geology. Programs in geophysical technology, geophysical engineering, geophysical prospecting, and engineering geology also offer related training for beginning geologists.

Traditional geoscience courses emphasize classical geologic methods and concepts. Mineralogy, paleontology, stratigraphy, and structural geology are important courses for undergraduates. Students interested in environmental and regulatory fields should take courses in hydrology, hazardous waste management, environmental legislation, chemistry, fluid mechanics, and geologic logging.

In addition, students should take courses in related sciences, mathematics, English composition, and computer science. Students seeking graduate degrees in geology concentrate on advanced courses in geology, placing major emphasis on their particular fields.

Other Requirements

In addition to academic training and work experience, geologists who work in the field or in administration must have skills in business administration and in working with other people. Computer modeling, data processing, and effective oral and written communication skills are important as are the ability to think independently and creatively. Physical stamina is needed for those involved in fieldwork.

Exploring

Students interested in a career in geology should read as much as possible about geology and geologists. It would also be helpful to take a college course in geology, such as mineralogy or physical geology.

A student's best chance for association with geologists and geological work is to join the clubs or organizations concerned with such things as rock collecting. Amateur geological groups and local museums also offer opportunities to gain exposure to the field of geology.

Employers

The majority of geologists are employed in private industry. Some work for oil and gas extraction and mining companies, primarily in exploration. The rest work for business service, environmental and geotechnical consulting firms, or are self-employed as consultants to industry and government. The federal government employs geologists in the Department of the Interior (in the U.S. Geological Survey, the Bureau of Mines, or the Bureau of Reclamation) and in the Departments of Defense, Agriculture, and Commerce. Geologists also work for state agencies, nonprofit research organizations, and museums. Many geologists hold faculty positions at colleges and universities and most of these combine their teaching with research.

Starting Out

After completing sufficient educational requirements, preferably a master's degree or doctorate, the geologist may look for work in various areas, including private industry and government. For those who wish to teach at the college level, a doctorate is required. College graduates may take government civil service examinations or possibly find work on state geological surveys, which are sometimes based on civil service competition.

Geologists often begin their careers in field exploration or as research assistants in laboratories. As they gain experience, they are given more difficult assignments and may be promoted to supervisory positions, such as project leader or program manager.

Advancement

The geologist with a bachelor's degree has little chance of advancing to higher-level positions. Continued formal training and work experience are necessary, especially as competition for these positions grows more intense. A doctorate is essential for most college or university teaching positions and is preferred for much research work.

Earnings

Beginning geologists earn about $30,900 a year on the average; those with master's and doctoral degrees earn more. However, starting salaries vary widely depending on the employing industry. For example, the average starting salary in the oil and gas industry is approximately $48,400 for those with bachelor's degrees, while geologists with bachelor's degrees employed in research institutions, colleges, and universities typically start out making less.

In the federal government, the average salary for geologists in managerial, supervisory, and nonsupervisory positions is about $59,700 a year; for geophysicists, $67,000; for hydrologists, $54,800; and for oceanographers, $62,700.

Although the petroleum, mineral, and mining industries offer higher salaries, competition for these jobs is stiff, and there is less job security than in other areas. In addition, college and university teachers can earn additional income through research, writing, and consulting. Salaries for foreign assignments may range significantly higher than those in the United States.

Work Environment

Some geologists spend most of their time in a laboratory or office, working a regular 40-hour week in pleasant conditions; others divide their time between fieldwork and office or laboratory work. Those who work in the field often travel to remote sites by helicopter or four-wheel drive vehicle and cover large areas on foot. They may camp for extended periods of time in primitive conditions with the members of the geological team as their only companions. *Exploration geologists* often work overseas or in remote areas, and job relocation is not unusual. *Geological oceanographers* may spend considerable time at sea.

Outlook

In response to the curtailed petroleum activity in the late 1980s and 1990s, the number of graduates in geology and geophysics, especially petroleum geology, dropped considerably in the last decade. Stability has now returned to the petroleum industry, increasing the need for qualified geoscientists. With new technologies and greater demand for energy resources, job opportunities are expected to be good, especially for those with a master's degree and for those familiar with computer modeling and GPS (global positioning system).

According to the *Occupational Outlook Handbook*, employment of geologists is expected to grow about as fast as the average for all occupations through the year 2006. In addition to the oil and gas industries, geologists will be able to find jobs in environmental protection and reclamation. Government agencies will have fewer jobs available because of cutbacks.

For More Information

For information on geoscientist careers, contact:

American Geological Institute
4220 King Street
Alexandria, VA 22302
Tel: 703-379-2480
Email: her@agiweb.org
Web: http://www.agiweb.org

For information on certification, contact:

American Institute of Professional Geologists
7828 Vance Drive, Suite 103
Arvada, CO 80003-2125
Tel: 303-431-0831
Email: aipg@aipg.org
Web: http://www.aipg.org

Association of Engineering Geologists
Department of Geology and Geophysics
Texas A&M University, MS-3115
College Station, TX 77843-3115
Tel: 409-845-0142
Web: http://aegweb.org

For career information and job listings, contact:

Geological Society of America
3300 Penrose Place
Boulder, CO 80301-9140
Tel: 303-447-2020
Email: educate@geosociety.org
Web: http://www.geosociety.org

Geophysicists

Overview

Geophysicists are concerned with matter and energy and how they interact. They study the physical properties and structure of the earth, from its interior to its upper atmosphere, including land surfaces, subsurfaces, and bodies of water.

History

Geophysics is an important field that combines the sciences of geology and physics. Geology is the study of the history and composition of the earth as recorded by rock formations and fossils. Physics deals with all forms of energy, the properties of matter, and the relationship between energy and matter. The geophysicist is an "earth physicist," one who works with the physical aspects of the earth from its inner core to outer space.

This alliance between the earth and physical sciences is part of the progress that science has made in searching for new understandings of the world. Like the fields of biochemistry, biomathematics, space medicine, and nuclear physics, geophysics combines the knowledge of two disciplines. However, the importance of geophysics goes well beyond abstract theory. Geophysicists apply their knowledge to such practical problems as predicting earthquakes, locating raw materials and sources of power, and evaluating sites for power plants.

The Job

Geophysicists use the principles and techniques of geology, physics, chemistry, mathematics, and engineering to perform tests and conduct research on the surface, atmosphere, waters, and solid bodies of the earth. They study seismic, gravitational, electrical, thermal, and magnetic phenomena to determine the structure and composition of the earth, as well as the forces causing movement and warping of the surface.

Many geophysicists are involved in fieldwork, where they engage in exploration and prospecting. Others work in laboratories, where research activities are the center of attention. In general, their instruments are highly complex and designed to take very precise measurements. Most geophysicists specialize in one of the following areas.

Geodesists measure the shape and size of the earth to determine fixed points, positions, and elevations on or near the earth's surface. Using the gravimeter, they perform surveys to measure minute variations in the earth's gravitational field. They also collect data that is useful in learning more about the weight, size, and mass of the earth. Geodesists are active in tracking satellites orbiting in outer space.

Geomagneticians use the magnetometer to measure variations in the earth's magnetic field from magnetic observatories and stations. They are also concerned with conditions affecting radio signals, solar phenomena, and many other aspects of space exploration. The data gathered can be most helpful in working with problems in radio and television transmission, telegraphy, navigation, mapping, and space exploration and space science.

Applied geophysicists use data gathered from the air and ground, as well as computers, to analyze the earth's crust. They look for oil and mineral deposits and try to find sites for the safe disposal of hazardous wastes.

Exploration geophysicists, sometimes called *geophysical prospectors,* use seismic techniques to look for possible oil and gas deposits. They may use sonar equipment to send sound waves deep into the earth. The resulting echo helps them estimate if an oil deposit lies hidden in the area.

Hydrologists are concerned with the surface and underground waters in the land areas of the earth. They map and chart the flow and the disposition of sediments; measure changes in water volume; and collect data on the form and intensity of precipitation, as well as on the disposition of water through evaporation and ground absorption. The information that the hydrologist collects is applied to problems in flood control, crop production, soil and water conservation, irrigation, and inland water projects. Some hydrologists study glaciers and their sedimentation.

Seismologists specialize in the study of earthquakes. With the aid of the seismograph and other instruments that record the location of earthquakes and the vibrations they cause, seismologists examine active fault lines and areas where earthquakes have occurred. They are often members of field teams whose purpose is to examine and evaluate possible building or construction sites. They also may explore for oil and minerals. In recent years, seismologists have contributed to the selection of missile launching sites.

Tectonophysicists study the structure of mountains and ocean basins, the properties of the earth's crust, and the physical forces and processes that cause movements and changes in the structure of the earth. A great deal of the work is research, and the findings are helpful in locating oil and mineral deposits.

Volcanologists study volcanoes, their location, and their activity. They are concerned with their origin and the phenomena of their processes.

Planetologists use data from artificial satellites and astronauts' equipment to study the makeup and atmosphere of the planets, the moon, and other bodies in our solar system. Recent advances in this field have greatly increased our knowledge of Jupiter, Saturn, and their satellites.

Requirements

High School

A strong interest in the physical and earth sciences is essential for this field. High school students should take basic courses in earth science, physics, chemistry, and at least four years of mathematics. Advanced placement work in any of the mathematics or sciences would also be helpful. Other recommended courses include mechanical drawing, shop, social studies, English, and computer science.

Postsecondary Training

A bachelor's degree in geophysics is required for most entry-level positions. Physics, mathematics, and chemistry majors can locate positions in geophysics, but some work in geology is highly desirable and often required, especially for certain government positions.

Graduate work at the master's or doctoral level is required for research and college teaching positions and for positions of a policy-making or policy-interpreting nature in private or government employment.

Many colleges and universities offer a bachelor's degree in geophysics, and a growing number of these institutions also award advanced degrees. An undergraduate major in geophysics is not usually required for entrance into a graduate program.

Other Requirements

Those who seek employment in the federal government will have to take a civil service examination and be able to meet other specified requirements.

A geophysicist should possess a strong aptitude in mathematics and science, particularly the physical and earth sciences, and an interest in observing nature, performing experiments, and studying the physical environment. Because geophysicists frequently spend time outdoors, it is helpful to enjoy such activities as hiking and camping.

Exploring

High school students can explore various aspects of this field in earth and physical science courses. Units of study dealing with electricity, rocks and minerals, metals and metallurgy, the universe and space, and weather and climate may offer an opportunity for further learning about the field. Hobbies that deal with radio, electronics, and rock or map collecting also offer opportunities to learn about the basic principles involved in geophysics.

Some colleges and universities have a chapter of the Society of Exploration Geophysicists that interested students can join. Employment as an aide or helper with a geophysical field party may be available during the summer months and provide students the opportunity to study the physical environment and interact with geophysicists.

Employers

Geophysicists are employed primarily by the petroleum industry, mining companies, exploration and consulting firms, and research institutions. A few geophysicists work as consultants, offering their services on a fee or contract basis. Many work for the federal government, mainly the Coast and Geodetic Survey, the U.S. Geological Survey, the Army Map Service, and the Naval Oceanographic Office. Other geophysicists pursue teaching careers.

Starting Out

Most college placement offices are prepared to help students locate positions in business, industry, or government agencies. Other job contacts can be made through professors, friends, or relatives. Some companies visit college campuses in the spring of each year to interview candidates who are interested in positions as geophysicists. The college placement office can usually provide helpful information on job opportunities in the field of geophysics.

Advancement

If employed by a private firm, a new employee with only a bachelor's degree will probably have an on-the-job training period. As a company trainee, the beginning geophysicist may be assigned to a number of different jobs. On a field party, the trainee will probably work with a *junior geophysicist*, which in many companies is the level of assignment received after the training has ended.

From a junior geophysicist, advancement is usually to *intermediate geophysicist*, and eventually to geophysicist. From this point, one can transfer to research positions, or if the geophysicist remains in fieldwork, to *party chief*.

The party chief's job is to coordinate the work of people in a crew, including trainees, junior, intermediate, and full geophysicists, surveyors, observers, drillers, shooters, and aides. Advancement with the company may eventually lead to supervisory and management positions.

Geophysicists can often transfer to other jobs in the fields of geology, physics, and engineering, depending on their qualifications and experience.

Earnings

The salaries of geophysicists are comparable to the earnings of those in other scientific professions. Most entry-level geophysicists with a bachelor's degree earn around $30,900 a year. Experienced geophysicists earn $59,700; higher level positions pay $90,000 or more. Additional compensation is awarded to those who are required to live outside the United States. The average salary for a geophysicist working for the federal government is $67,100.

Both the federal government and private industry provide additional benefits, including vacations, retirement pensions, health and life insurance, and sick leave benefits.

Positions in colleges and universities offer annual salaries ranging from about $28,000 for instructors to $65,000 for full professors. Salaries depend upon experience, education, and professional rank. Faculty members may teach in summer school for additional compensation and also engage in writing, consulting, and research for government, industry, or business.

Work Environment

Geophysicists employed in laboratories or offices generally work a regular 40-hour week under typical office conditions. Field geophysicists work under a variety of conditions and often the hours are irregular. They are outdoors much of the time in all kinds of weather. The work requires carrying small tools and equipment and occasionally some heavy lifting. The field geophysicist is often required to travel and work in isolated areas. Volcanologists, for example, may face dangerous conditions when visiting and gathering data near an erupting volcano.

Outlook

According to the *Occupational Outlook Handbook*, employment of geophysicists is expected to grow about as fast as the average through the year 2006. The total number of graduates with degrees in geophysical sciences is expected to remain small and insufficient to meet the moderate increase in industry job openings. This may eventually result in fewer employment possibilities in college teaching.

Although the petroleum industry, the largest employer of geophysicists, has cut back on its exploration activities, more geophysicists will be needed to locate less accessible fuel and mineral deposits and to do research on such problems as radioactivity, cosmic and solar radiation, and the use of geothermal energy to generate electricity. The petroleum industry is also expected to expand operations overseas, which may create new jobs for those who are willing to travel.

The federal government will need more geophysicists to study water, conservation, flood control, and other problems and to assist in space science projects. The growing need to find new sources of energy will undoubtedly make the work of geophysicists more important and more challenging in the next century.

For More Information

For information on geoscientist careers, contact:

American Geological Institute
4220 King Street
Alexandria, VA 22302
Tel: 703-379-2480
Web: http://www.agiweb.org

The following organization holds regular meetings and publishes findings.

American Geophysical Union
2000 Florida Avenue, NW
Washington, DC 20009
Tel: 202-462-6900
Web: http://www.agu.org

This society offers an annual exposition, networking, and continuing education opportunities. It also has student chapters at colleges and universities.

Society of Exploration Geophysicists
PO Box 702740
Tulsa, OK 74170
Tel: 918-497-5500
Web: http://seg.org

Groundwater Professionals

Earth science Mathematics Physics	School Subjects
Technical/scientific	Personal Skills
Indoors and outdoors Primarily one location	Work Environment
Bachelor's degree	Minimum Education Level
$25,000 to $30,000 to $60,000+	Salary Range
Voluntary	Certification or Licensing
About as fast as the average	Outlook

Overview

The title *groundwater professional* is a blanket name for a number of different types of scientists and engineers concerned with water supplies beneath the earth's surface.

History

In addition to the water that can be seen on the surface of the earth—lakes, streams, rivers, ponds, canals, oceans—there is water under the ground, known as groundwater. Groundwater includes things like underground streams and aquifers, which are layers of water-bearing porous rock or sediment. People have been tapping into various groundwater sources for centuries, using it for everything from drinking water to irrigation.

Artesian wells, for example, are used to provide water (including drinking water) to some parts of the world. They are created by boring down into aquifers, with the resulting pressure causing water in the aquifer to rise up in the well. Australia has the world's biggest artesian well system; in the United States, artesian systems supply water to parts of the Great Plains and the East Coast.

Like other natural resources, groundwater has been the focus of increasing attention in the United States since the 1970s. The U.S. government has recognized threats to this vital supply of water and passed laws to protect it. At first, people in the field and in related fields were called on to adapt their skills to meeting the new regulations. In recent years, especially as the regulations have gotten more technical and complex, demand for people who specialize in groundwater science has risen dramatically.

A look at the groundwater situation in one state, Florida, demonstrates some of the potential problems. The groundwater in many areas is located not very far under the surface—just a few feet, in some cases. A surging population is drawing heavily on these supplies, threatening to use them faster than they can replenish themselves. Rapid development (farming, mining, construction, industry) offers high potential for disrupting the vulnerable groundwater.

Also, in some cases, below the aquifers in Florida that carry good water are aquifers that carry poor-quality water, high in sulfates. Drawing down too far into the aquifers that have good water might accidentally pull up the bad water from the aquifer below it—or, worse, pull over saltwater from the coast. Once saltwater gets in, that aquifer is probably lost as a source of drinking water.

There are other hazards as well. When there is a fuel, chemical, or other spill on the ground, the hazardous chemicals in these substances can soak through the soil and reach the groundwater, contaminating it. Even good-quality groundwater usually is treated before it is used (although in some places, like outlying rural areas, people drink untreated groundwater, drawing it right out of the ground). Regular water treatment facilities are not designed to handle removal of hazardous substances. That requires special steps, is usually more difficult and expensive than cleaning surface water, and sometimes does not work.

This is, in fact, a national concern. Today, some 53 percent of the United States relies on groundwater for its drinking water. At the same time, better methods for detecting contaminants have revealed that contamination of groundwater is more extensive than was known before.

Legislation—including the Resource Conservation and Recovery Act (RCRA), the Comprehensive Environmental Response, Compensation, and Liability Act (CERCLA), the Superfund Amendments and Reauthorization Act (SARA), and the Safe Drinking Water Act (SDWA)—mandates the cleanup, monitoring, and protection of the nation's groundwater supplies. This direction was strengthened by later amendments to such laws. Recent stricter regulations applying to landfills, for example, acknowledge the potential risks of these operations to groundwater. In particular, seepage from landfills can get into the groundwater and contaminate it. New landfills must have double liners and other features to help prevent seepage; existing landfills have new rules about closing and capping the landfill to try to stop or minimize seepage. Groundwater monitoring equipment is used to take constant readings of the area's groundwater and determine if any seepage is occurring.

The special problems of groundwater, people's reliance on it, and the laws passed to protect it all have contributed to the growing need for groundwater professionals. No one really has the title "groundwater professional"; instead, it describes any of a number of different positions within the groundwater industry. These include different types of scientists, engineers, and technicians employed in government, private industry, and nonprofit organizations at various tasks designed to ensure safe, effective, and lawful use of groundwater supplies. In earlier times, *geologists* were often called upon to do groundwater work, and they continue to be important players in the field today. Geology is the science of the earth's history, composition, and structure. Specialties in the groundwater field today include hydrogeology and hydrology. Hydrogeology is the science of groundwater supplies. Hydrology is the study of water and its properties, including how water is distributed on earth and how it moves through land. Other professionals in the groundwater industry include chemists, geological engineers, water quality technicians, computer modelers, *environmental engineers,* chemists, bioremediation specialists, petroleum geologists, and mining engineers.

Groundwater work is part of the water quality management segment of the environmental industry, which accounts for about one-quarter of all spending on the environment, according to the Environmental Careers Organization (ECO).

The Job

Employers of groundwater professionals include local water districts, government agencies, consulting firms, landfill operations, private industry, and others with a stake in successful groundwater management. What groundwater professionals do depends on their employers and what their pressing concerns are.

For example, local or regional authorities usually are responsible for ensuring a safe and adequate water supply for people in the area. A groundwater professional might help with permitting work: any time people want to make a new use of water or do something that might affect water in the area (like building a road, drilling a well, or laying a sewer), they have to get a permit. Before it will issue a permit, the authority checks the site and decides if the use is safe. Typically, geologists do the necessary fieldwork, while engineers handle the actual obtaining of permits.

For a local or regional authority, groundwater professionals might help locate new sources of water in the area. That typically involves surveying the area, drilling for samples, and measuring the capacity of any water reserves found. They also might find the source of the groundwater and determine its ability to replenish itself if tapped for use; decide how the water would best be used; and make a recommendation to the authority. If the authority approves, a new well system is designed to tap the groundwater, and wells are drilled.

States are big employers of groundwater professionals. What a groundwater professional would do for a state depends greatly on what part of the country it is in. Most states have a strategy for managing their groundwater. The mapping of known groundwater supplies, often using computer modeling to show groundwater flow and possible effects of contamination, is often part of their efforts.

For both state and local or regional authorities, combating the effects of contamination is a critical task. The nature and extent of contamination, combined with the geologic and hydrologic characteristics of the surrounding land, determine whether the water supply is permanently tainted or can be made usable again in the future. Groundwater professionals might design systems to reduce or stop contamination.

Other major employers are consulting firms. Regulations for waste treatment and disposal are becoming stricter and stricter, and that means that more technical expertise is required. Lacking that expertise themselves, many waste generators in the public and private sectors turn to consulting firms for help. Consultants may be called in to help with a hazardous waste cleanup around a landfill, at a Superfund site (an abandoned hazardous waste site), or at another cleanup; they may help a private industrial company devise a system to handle its waste. Groundwater professionals can be very useful to such consulting firms. For example, if a landfill is leaking waste into a source of groundwater, the groundwater specialist may be asked to devise solutions, such as digging new drainage systems for the landfill or building new containment facilities. A groundwater professional with a consulting firm might work close to home or travel to job sites around the country, or even around the world. The field of groundwater management is evolving rapidly, so employment figures quickly become obsolete. However, in one survey by the Association of Ground Water Scientists and Engineers (AGWSE), a division of the National Ground Water Association, nearly half of respondents worked for private consulting firms. About 24 percent worked for regional, state, county, or municipal governments. The rest were employed by the federal government, teaching or research institutions, or other employers.

Requirements

High School

At the high school level, you can prepare for a career in groundwater work by taking a lot of science and math. High technology is important in this field, so hone your computer skills. Finally, focus on developing your writing and speech skills as well. Reports, proposals, memos, scientific papers, and other forms of written and verbal communication are highly likely to be part of your job as a groundwater professional.

Postsecondary Training

A bachelor's degree is the minimum requirement for being a professional in this field. According to ECO, geology, civil engineering, and chemistry are the most common undergraduate degrees in this field today. Other appropriate majors are engineering geology, hydrogeology, geophysics, petroleum geology, mining engineering, and other related degrees. Another possibility is a degree in hydrology, although it is not currently offered by many schools. Appropriate course work at the undergraduate level includes chemistry, physics, calculus, groundwater geology, groundwater hydrology, engineering hydrology, and fluid mechanics. It is also a good idea to learn how to do computer modeling, mapping, and related tasks. Undergraduate degrees are good for getting a job doing things like on-site sampling and measurement.

A degree in hydrogeology is something usually obtained at the master's level. This degree and some experience will place you among the most sought-after workers in the environmental industry, according to ECO.

Almost two-thirds of the people responding to the AGWSE survey had earned master's degrees, and 11 percent had earned a doctorate.

Certification or Licensing

Some certification programs have been developed to measure experience and knowledge of groundwater science. Both the American Institute of Hydrology and the Association of Ground Water Scientists and Engineers (a division of the National Groundwater Association) offer certification programs.

Other Requirements

Patience, persistence, curiosity, attention to detail, and good analyzing skills would all be useful for a groundwater professional. You would be likely to work as part of a team and have people to answer to, whether a supervisor, the government, a client, or all three. You would also probably have to be familiar with many regulations, often complex ones.

Exploring

You should hold one or more internships while in college (check with your college department for opportunities). You also might be able to find a part-time or summer job with a consulting firm. In addition, check into research opportunities with your professors at your school. You may be able to earn a small salary while gaining experience in fieldwork, compiling and interpreting data, or computer modeling. Volunteering for a nonprofit environmental organization might also be an option.

Employers

Employers of groundwater professionals include local water districts, government agencies, consulting firms, landfill operations, private industry, and others with a stake in successful groundwater management.

Starting Out

There are many ways to find openings in the industry. One obvious place to start is the want ads, both in the daily newspaper and in various professional journals. Local chapters of groundwater and geological societies sometimes have lists of job opportunities or bulletin boards with important notices. New graduates can also look for work at state employment offices, local or regional water authorities, or the local branches of federal agencies.

Advancement

With an undergraduate degree, you are likely to start out doing activites such as sampling and measuring work. What it takes to advance depends on your employer but probably will include some years of experience plus an advanced degree. It is advisable to keep up on the latest developments in the field through seminars, workshops, and other courses.

In a private consulting firm, you might be promoted to an administrative position, where you would spend more time in the office, deal with clients, and direct the activities of other groundwater specialists and office staff. For a local, regional, state, or federal organization, you may rise to an administrative level, where you would meet with planning commissions, public interest groups, legislative bodies, and industry groups.

Another option is to strike out on your own. With some experience, ambitious professionals might start their own consulting firms.

Earnings

Groundwater professionals earn salaries in the upper range of those for all water industry professionals. Entry-level jobs with local authorities start in the mid-$20,000 range, with state and federal authorities closer to $30,000 and private-sector employers from $30,000 and up. Midrange salaries are about $30,000 to $40,000. Managers can earn $60,000 and up.

Respondents to AGWSE's survey reported an average salary of $38,250. More than three-quarters of them earned between $25,000 and $50,000 annually.

Benefits depend on the employer. They might include paid vacation, sick days, personal days, health and dental insurance, tuition reimbursement, retirement savings plans, use of company vehicles, and the like.

Work Environment

Fieldwork might mean going out into natural areas to survey the geophysical characteristics of a site. You might take groundwater samples from the monitoring wells near a gas station, fuel storage facility, landfill, sewage treatment plant, or manufacturing company. You might oversee the digging of a new well system or stop in to see how a new well system is running. It depends on your specific job.

Instead of (or in addition to) fieldwork, you may work in an office. Conditions in offices vary by employer, but the offices are generally equipped with state-of-the-art technology. Most groundwater professionals work a 40-hour week, although this may vary depending on project deadlines or unexpected developments in the field.

Outlook

Like many environmental occupations, groundwater career opportunities surged in the 1980s in response to stricter government regulations. The field continued to grow through the mid-1990s but now is beginning to level off. Jim Lundy, a hydrogeologist employed by the Minnesota Pollution Control Agency, comments, "The field was burgeoning in the 1980s. I don't know whether we'll ever see growth like that again, but the field isn't going to contract severely either. As long as people continue to need water, there will be a need for groundwater professionals."

While this field may not be growing as rapidly today as it was five to ten years ago, it remains a promising career choice for motivated, intelligent students. The continued growth of our nation's population will make finding and remediating groundwater supplies an even more pressing issue in the next century. Amendments to the Resource Conservation and Recovery Act, the Clean Water Act, and other legislation signal that groundwater is a priority to the government. Private industry needs to comply with stricter regulations, including those related to keeping groundwater safe from contamination. Local, regional, and state authorities need to map, develop, and protect their groundwater supplies. Consultants need the specific expertise that groundwater professionals can offer, for clients both in the United States and abroad. Research is needed to develop new ways to treat contaminated groundwater, to prevent spills or leaks, and to develop systems that will make the most of groundwater supplies. All of this means work for groundwater professionals for the near future.

For More Information

The following organization's publications include Careers in Geology *and* Directory of Geoscience Departments:

American Geological Institute
4220 King Street
Alexandria, VA 22302-1502
Tel: 703-379-2480
Email: agi@agiweb.org
Web: http://www.agiweb.org

The AGU's magazine Earth in Space *is designed for use by teachers in the classroom. The cost is about $26 for the school year.*

American Geophysical Union
2000 Florida Avenue, NW
Washington, DC 20009-1277
Tel: 800-966-2481
Email: service@agu.org
Web: http://earth.agu.org

Young people interested in hydrology can write to the following organization for a brochure published by the University Council on Water Resources, a nonprofit organization, and for information on certification.

American Institute of Hydrology
2499 Rice Street, Suite 135
St. Paul, MN 55113-3724
Tel: 651-484-8169
Email: aihydro@aol.com
Web: http://www.aihydro.org

Members of this society include geological technicians, geologists, paleontologists, and petrologists:

The Geological Society of America
PO Box 9140
3300 Penrose Place
Boulder, CO 80301-9140
Tel: 303-447-2020
Email: member@geosociety.org
Web: http://www.geosociety.org

For information on certification, contact:

National Ground Water Association
601 Dempsey Road
Westerville, OH 43081
Tel: 800-551-7379
Email: ngwa@ngwa.org
Web: http://www.ngwa.org

Hazardous Waste Management Specialists

Biology Chemistry	School Subjects
Technical/scientific Mechanical/manipulative	Personal Skills
Indoors and outdoors Primarily multiple locations	Work Environment
Bachelor's degree	Minimum Education Level
$26,000 to $38,000 to $51,000+	Salary Range
Required by certain states	Certification or Licensing
Faster than the average	Outlook

Overview

The title *hazardous waste management specialist* encompasses a group of people who do one or more of the following: identify hazardous waste, ensure safe handling and disposal, and work to reduce generation of hazardous waste. There are about 90,000 hazardous waste management specialists employed in the United States today. Because their duties vary so widely, hazardous waste management specialists may work for a number of different employers, from producers of hazardous waste such as industry, hospitals, and utilities to government agencies who monitor these producers. They may also work for the solid waste or public health departments of local governments.

History

Today, hazardous waste management specialists oversee the handling of hundreds of substances the government identifies as hazardous to human health or the environment. However, this was not always the case. Prior to World War II, "hazardous waste" consisted of pesticides, which were under the regulation of the Food and Drug Administration, as well as by-products from a few industrial processes. Scientists and engineers who worked for the FDA or private industry monitored the disposal of these wastes to the minimal extent required. Before the environmental boom in the late 1960s, these wastes were handled much like regular garbage, dumped directly into open waterways, buried in landfills, and stored or buried in 55-gallon drums at the industrial site.

With the emergence of the Nuclear Age came a new waste that no one seemed to know how to handle: radioactive waste. This waste presented unique challenges because of its insidious nature; it is generally colorless and odorless and remains hazardous for hundreds of years. Government scientists and engineers were the first to work on proper disposal with utilities that produced such waste (nuclear power plants). Today, hazardous waste management specialists work with these professionals on the handling of radioactive waste.

Postwar America also saw the beginnings of widespread use of synthetic materials: as one advertisement from the 1950s put it, America could enjoy "better living through chemistry." Unfortunately, this improvement also had a darker side: the tons of chemical wastes that chemical industries produced, in addition to some of the products themselves, were to have adverse and long-lasting effects on health and the environment that no one foresaw. Crude oil gushing from Union Oil Company's Platform A covered beaches in Santa Barbara in early 1969; only five months later the Cuyahoga River in Ohio caught fire. Public outrage directed at environmental disaster after disaster signaled the end of such cavalier practices.

During the flurry of environmentally directed legislation in the 1970s, hazardous waste was not considered different from other types of pollution. The Resource Conservation and Recovery Act of 1976 (RCRA) gave the fledgling Environmental Protection Agency (EPA) power to assign permits for waste production and disposal, to track waste, to inspect facilities, and to fine offenders for noncompliance. That same year, the Toxic Substance Control Act (TSCA) forced manufacturers to submit formal notifications before they started commercially producing substances that could be toxic. Four criteria determine whether waste is hazardous: toxicity, ignitability, corrosivity, and reactivity.

This spate of legislation was thought to cover all aspects of hazardous substance management. But as the citizens of Love Canal found in 1978, this wasn't exactly the case. A rash of sickness there triggered an investigation that uncovered 21,900 tons of chemical wastes buried in 55-gallon drums that had leaked into basements of houses and the local public school. The resulting publicity led to the discovery of thousands of similar sites throughout the United States. The Comprehensive Environmental Response, Compensation, and Liability Act of 1980 (CERCLA) was the political response to the furor surrounding these environmental crises.

CERCLA, or Superfund as it came to be known, is a government fund that selects and pays for cleanup of abandoned, inoperative contaminated sites. Superfund also monitors new spills. Superfund established a National Priorities List of thousands of the worst sites, giving a budget and a timeline for completion of cleanup at these sites. In 1985, after a lukewarm beginning, Superfund was strengthened by the Superfund Amendment and Reauthorization Act (SARA). SARA expanded the environmental cleanup budget, allowed for civil suits against violators of the acts, and gave the EPA standards and deadlines to meet. Superfund undergoes constant review and evolution: some companies hire individuals whose jobs consist solely of tracking Superfund and associated legislative changes.

Superfund is only one example of how opportunities have grown for people who specialize in the handling of hazardous waste. The evolution of environmental awareness has created jobs for people who can handle hazardous wastes that vary from monitoring leachate from municipal landfills to gases emitted from industrial smokestacks to chemicals buried years ago all over the United States.

The Job

Management of hazardous waste in the United States is handled in a variety of ways. Specialists may work anywhere along the continuum of hazardous waste management, preventing spills or contamination before they happen, helping to control them when they do, identifying contaminated sites that have existed for years, and cleaning up and disposing of hazardous waste.

Not all of the hazardous waste management specialist's time is spent in the field or in the lab. Because management of hazardous waste is highly regulated, hazardous waste management specialists are involved in a substantial amount of record-keeping and paperwork. The cleanup of a contaminated site, for example, may take several months or even years. There is a bureaucratic process that must be followed. An example of steps a hazardous waste management specialist may be involved in before any cleanup proceeds includes: 1) identification of the hazardous substance and testing to gauge the extent of contamination; 2) search for or negotiation with parties responsible for the contamination; 3) development of a plan of how best to clean up the site and how much it may cost; 4) waiting for several months or longer for approval and funding to clean up the site; and 5) public hearings to notify how, why, and when the cleanup will be done.

Because for many years hazardous waste was simply dumped anywhere, contaminated sites exist everywhere. Before hazardous waste laws such as SARA and Superfund were passed, for example, a paint manufacturer might have innocently dumped mounds of garbage containing toxic substances into a nearby field. Today, that dump may be leaking hazardous substances into the surrounding groundwater, which nearby communities use for drinking. Specialists study the site and determine what hazardous substances are involved, how bad the damage is, and what can be done to remove the waste and restore the site. They suggest strategies for the cleanup within legal, economic, and other constraints. Once the cleanup is underway, teams of specialists help ensure the waste is removed and the site properly restored. Some specialists supervise *hazardous waste management technicians,* who do the sampling, monitoring, and testing at suspect sites.

Specialists who work for emergency response companies help stop or control accidental spills and leaks of hazardous waste, such as those that can occur when a tank truck containing gasoline is involved in an accident. Specialists working for hospitals or other producers of medical wastes help determine how to safely dispose of such wastes. Those working for research institutes or other small generators of radioactive materials advise employers about handling or storing materials.

Government-employed hazardous waste management specialists often perform general surveys of past and ongoing projects, assemble comparative cost analyses of different remedial procedures, and make recommendations for the regulation of new hazardous wastes. Government hazardous waste management specialists make detailed analyses of hazardous waste sites, known as Remedial Investigation and Feasibility Studies (RI/FS). Using data provided by technicians and other support personnel, these hazardous waste specialists weigh economic, environmental, legal, political, and social factors and devise a remediation (cleanup) plan that best suits a particular site. Some help develop hazardous waste management laws.

Other specialists work in pollution control and risk assessment for private companies. They help hazardous waste-producing firms limit their waste output, decrease the likelihood of emergency situations, maintain compliance with federal regulations, and even modify their processes to eliminate hazardous waste altogether. Hazardous waste management specialists might also help develop processes that utilize potential waste.

Requirements

High School

High school students interested in preparing for careers as hazardous waste management specialists need to be strong in chemistry and other sciences such as biology and geology. English and other communications classes will aid aspiring specialists in college and will help them to effectively present their findings in their professional pursuits.

Postsecondary Training

Although some specialists enter this field with undergraduate degrees in engineering—environmental, chemical, or civil—it is not strictly necessary for the work involved. Many employers in this field train their employees with the help of technical institutes or community colleges with courses on hazardous waste disposal. A bachelor's degree in environmental resource management, chemistry, geology, or ecology also may be acceptable. Areas of expertise such as hydrology or subsurface hydrology may require a master's or doctoral degree.

Certification or Licensing

Certification available to specialists is not universally recognized, and requirements for certification vary not only from state to state, but region to region, and year to year as well. After some years in the field, hazardous waste management professionals can gain certification through associations such as the National Environmental Health Association in Denver. Training for this certification can be obtained through job experience or coursework provided by a number of institutes and community colleges nationwide. Some employers pay for workshops run in-house by these institutes to update their employees on such topics as emergency response, Superfund regulations, and emerging technologies. Although certification is not required, it lends weight to recommendations made by government-employed specialists and generally enhances a specialist's credibility.

Other Requirements

The relative newness of this field, its dependence on political support, the varied nature of its duties, and its changing regulations and technologies all require a large degree of flexibility from hazardous waste management specialists. The ability to take into consideration the many economic, environmental, legal, and social aspects of each project is key, as are thoroughness and patience in completing the necessary work. Prospective employers look for job candidates with excellent communications skills, no matter what their specialty, as this position is so reliant on the shared information of numerous professionals.

Exploring

Those who would like to explore avenues of hazardous waste management can get involved in local chapters of citizen watchdog groups and become familiar with nearby Superfund sites. What is being done at those sites? Who is responsible for the cleanup? What effect does the site have on its community? The Citizens Clearinghouse for Hazardous Waste, founded by Love Canal resident Lois Marie Gibbs, may be able to provide information about current concerns of citizens (see listing at the end of this article). A book written by Gibbs, *Love Canal: My Story*, details illnesses suffered by Love Canal residents and their frustration at difficulty in finding someone to take responsibility for the mess. *Love Canal: My Story* illustrates how the job of hazardous waste management specialist can make a difference in citizens' lives.

Additionally, understanding the problems of hazardous waste management and the controversy surrounding some of the limitations of Superfund provide a more detailed picture of the specialist's job. There are numerous magazines published on hazardous waste management, including those addressing the different waste generators and involved professionals—for example, chemical manufacturers, oil industry representatives, engineers, and conservationists. A few publications are *Integrated Waste Management*, *Journal of Environmental Quality*, and *Journal of Natural Resources and Life Sciences Education*. Outreach programs sponsored by the Army Corps of Engineers offer presentations to high schools in some areas and may be arranged with the help of science departments and placement office staff members.

Employers

Hazardous waste management specialists have opportunities with many types of employers. Federal, state, and local governments use hazardous waste management specialists in a variety of roles. On the local level, a hazardous waste management specialist may work within the public health, wastewater treatment, or municipal solid waste department, enforcing local regulations and overseeing disposal of hazardous waste. Hazardous waste management specialists employed by the federal government generally have a regulatory role, overseeing the cleanup of past contamination and ensuring subsequent contaminations don't occur by monitoring those who generate waste. Hazardous waste professionals in government tend to have health and safety backgrounds. In the private sector, some specialists work for several companies as independent consultants. Still other specialists are employed by citizen groups and environmental organizations to provide technical knowledge about environmental and safety hazards that may not warrant Superfund attention but still concern citizens who may be affected by them.

Starting Out

Employers in this field prefer hazardous waste management applicants with hands-on experience. Volunteering is one good way to acquire this experience and gauge the field to find a suitable niche. Internships are available through the Environmental Careers Organization (ECO), local nonprofit groups, and the EPA, among others. On-site experience at this level usually amounts to being a technician of sorts—running tests, preparing samples, and compiling data. Internships may pay minimal salaries, but most employers prefer candidates with even this kind of experience over applicants who have never seen how their education applies to real situations. Recent graduates and working professionals find jobs through trade association advertisements and on the Internet. Openings with government agencies can be found on the Web page of the Office of Personnel Management at http://www.usajobs.opm.gov or by calling 912-757-3000.

Those who are still in school can start building a background now by attending public meetings in their area concerning hazardous waste. Read your local newspaper or call city hall or county government to find out what the local issues are. Citizen action groups that advocate environmental awareness are another good place to learn what the issues are in your area and perhaps volunteer your time.

Advancement

To advance, hazardous waste management specialists need to be proficient in several aspects of hazardous waste management and be able to handle an entire hazardous waste site or group of similar sites. This involves supervising other specialists, engineers, laboratory chemists, and various support personnel as well as being the party responsible for reporting to regulatory agencies. Other specialists may find positions in public relations fields or higher management levels. Still others may seek further formal education and advance upon completion of higher degrees of specialization. The field of hazardous waste management is diverse, and after specialists have worked for a while, the range of specialties available will become more evident.

Earnings

Hazardous waste management specialists who enter the field with no experience earned around $26,000 per year in 1996; those who had experience as an intern or technician started at around $38,000, according to the Princeton Review. Some 75 percent of hazardous waste workers are employed by the private sector, with middle-range salaries averaging between $40,000 and $50,000 per year. Specialists with degrees in areas of high demand, such as toxicology or hydrology, can earn $80,000 or more, depending on seniority and certification levels. Specialists who obtain entry-level jobs with the government generally enter under the civil service classifications of GS-5 and GS-7 levels. In 1998, starting pay under the government's General Schedule was $19,969 for GS-5 and $24,734 for GS-7. However, the government notes that most of these jobs actually pay 5 to 12 percent more on average when adjusted for geographic location.

Specialists in the public and private sectors also enjoy benefits such as full health plans, vacation time, and subsidized travel arrangements. Employer-paid training is a common benefit in this field as regulations and technology are constantly evolving and employers want specialists who are up-to-date.

Work Environment

The complexity of the regulations often makes remediation work painstakingly slow, but also provides a measure of job security. High-publicity sites may bring considerable political and social pressure to bear on those responsible for their cleanup, especially if work appears to be moving very slowly. Competition for lucrative contracts can be fierce, and considerable effort must be made by employer and employee alike to stay abreast of changing technologies and legislation in order to be at the cutting edge of the field. The job of a specialist may require on-site exposure to hazardous wastes, and protective clothing that can hamper work efforts is often necessary. On the other end of the spectrum, there is always paperwork waiting to be completed back at the office. However, individuals in this field report a sense of accomplishment, and satisfaction in the field is extremely high. For some, the new developments that are a major part of the job provide welcome change and challenges.

Outlook

ECO calls hazardous waste management a "hot" environmental career and calls for individuals with specific technical skills who can also see the big picture. As with some other highly skilled environmental professions, hazardous waste management is currently suffering from a lack of qualified professionals. The sheer enormity of the hazardous waste problem, with over 40,000 known sites and more expected to be identified in the near future, ensures that there will be cleanup jobs available as long as funding is available. An environmental careers survey recorded in the *Engineering News Record* cautions, "Though there's still a lot of hazardous waste to clean up, it's anyone's guess as to when it will be done." Despite this, the mid-1990s have seen a higher-than-average growth rate for hazardous waste management professionals, and that trend is expected to continue for at least the next decade. ECO advises students to plan for changes in the field; whereas the current emphasis is on waste removal, neutralization, and disposal, future job markets will revolve around waste prevention. Keeping track of trends in the field while still in school will enable students to tailor their educations to the anticipated needs of the future job market.

For More Information

The following is a national grassroots organization founded by Lois Marie Gibbs and other Love Canal activists. It offers publications on environmental health and community organization:

Citizens Clearinghouse for Hazardous Waste (CCHW)
PO Box 6806
Falls Church, VA 22040
Tel: 703-237-2249
Web: http://www.essential.org/orgs/cchw

The following association provides certification for hazardous waste specialists:

National Environmental Health Association
720 South Colorado Boulevard
Denver, CO 80222
Tel: 303-756-9090
Web: http://www.neha.org

For information on hazardous waste management training and degree programs nationwide, contact:

National Partnership for Environmental Technology in Education (PETE)
6601 Owens Drive, Suite 235
Pleasanton, CA 94588
Tel: 510-225-0668

The following is a branch of the military that employs engineering professionals in hazardous waste management projects such as Superfund remediation sites:

U.S. Army Corps of Engineers
Massachusetts Avenue, NW
Washington, DC 20314-1000
Tel: 202-761-0010
Web: http://www.usace.army.mil/

Land Acquisition Professionals

Business Earth science	School Subjects
Communication/ideas Leadership/management	Personal Skills
Indoors and Outdoors One location with some travel	Work Environment
Bachelor's degree	Minimum Education Level
$20,000 to $33,000 to $40,000+	Salary Range
None available	Certification or Licensing
Faster than the average	Outlook

Overview

Land acquisition professionals assist in efforts of nonprofit land trusts to preserve land and water from development, subdivision, overly heavy recreational or agricultural use, or other human disruption by handling the land transaction—buying the land outright, acquiring development rights to it, obtaining easements, getting landowners to donate the land, or similar actions.

History

Land acquisitions has evolved as a specialty within nonprofit land trusts, which in turn are a special part of land and water conservation efforts in this country.

Land and water conservation efforts in the United States go back more than one hundred years, when the federal government first started setting aside wilderness areas and other open land and water. Since then, hundreds of millions of acres have been preserved in federally owned and managed national parks, wildlife refuges, wild and scenic rivers, and other areas as well as state or locally managed protected lands. Today, acquisition by the federal government is largely done. But acquisitions by private land trusts continue.

Broadly, land trusts are private nonprofit groups formed to acquire and manage open lands for the public's benefit. The first official one in this country was the Trustees of Reservations, formed in Boston in 1891. Concerned that open lands around the city were being rapidly swallowed up by development, this group of private citizens took action: they bought up some land themselves and made it available to the public for recreation.

Interest in the United States really took off in the 1960s and 1970s with those decades' increased public interest in the environment. Today, there are more than 1,000 private nonprofit land trusts, ranging from small, one- or two-person trusts to large statewide groups with paid staffs of 30 or more people.

There also are several large national land trust organizations that do land trust work themselves or provide support services to other land trusts. One is The Nature Conservancy (TNC), based in Arlington, Virginia, with state chapters nationwide. Established in the early 1950s, today it employs about 1,800 people (2,000 including contract and seasonal workers) and emphasizes conservation of "rare or relatively rare" species and natural communities. Sometimes this means acquiring or helping to acquire the land, according to media relations manager Juanita Thigpen. "We might raise money and buy a piece of property," she says. "We might work with landowners to get them to deed the land to us or to do a conservation easement, such as an agricultural or environmental easement."

Another key group is the Trust for Public Land (TPL) in San Francisco, established in the 1970s. An early TPL success was buying up miles of San Francisco coastline, rescuing it from developers' hands. (These areas now are managed by the National Park Service.) Today, TPL also provides a wide range of services to other land trusts, from an informational newsletter to help with handling land transactions.

The Land Trust Alliance was set up in 1982 by trusts nationwide that wanted a central organization in Washington, DC. In addition to providing information services, publications, documents, case studies, and other support to land trusts, it has a lobbyist to give land trusts a presence on Capitol Hill.

Trustees of Reservations—that first U.S. land trust—still exists today, according to Roe, and is still acquiring land statewide. In fact, Massachusetts has the largest number of land trusts of all the states, with "little land trust organizations in every town," he says. But land trusts also exist in every other state, too, doing their part to help keep forests, prairies, coastlines, and other areas intact.

The Job

Depending on the land trust, land acquisition may be one person's entire job, or it may be one task among many for an executive director or other employee. Larger, well-funded land trusts and national land trust organizations are most likely to have acquisitions professionals devoted solely to handling land transactions. This is true of TNC chapters, for example. "In a large chapter, like the California regional office, there may be one person devoted to land acquisition," says Thigpen. "In a smaller one, like Utah, one person may do everything from land acquisition to walking the land to fund-raising."

In any case, a group wishing to save some land or water has important questions to answer. Who owns it? Would they be willing to donate the land? If not, will they sell it? For how much? Who'll pay for it? Will a public agency buy it? Could a community group raise the needed funds?

A land trust can check with the local government to see if it's interested in helping to acquire the land. If that doesn't work, the trust can act on its own, trying to talk the landowner into selling or donating the land, for example. Or it can turn to big groups like the Land Trust Alliance, TNC, or TPL for help. At TPL, for example, project managers are available to help coordinate acquisitions efforts for other land trusts.

Generally, acquisitions involve either buying the land outright, acquiring development rights to it, obtaining easements, or getting landowners to donate the land or leave it to the land trust in their wills. Such negotiations usually don't go through the courts, explains Chuck Basset, vice president of human resources for TNC, but they do "go through a legal process," he says. Buying land, for example, typically involves "all the steps you'd follow when buying a house, like getting an appraisal and getting the title or deed." The land then becomes the property of the land trust.

For land donations, nonprofits offer certain advantages to landowners over donating to government or quasi-government groups. "Most land trusts are 501(c)3 nonprofit organizations," says Roe. "Generally, anything donated to a nonprofit is tax deductible." Large landowners may gain certain additional tax benefits by willing the land to a nonprofit when the landowner dies.

"In general, most government agencies are not set up to receive donations of land," Roe adds. "They're not flexible enough to deal with landowners like nonprofits are." Landowners also may like the nonprofits' conservation emphasis and may not like the idea of donating their land to the government, he says.

Instead of selling, donating, or willing the land, landowners might instead agree to easements that effectively put part of the land off-limits to development, subdivision, or other actions that might threaten preservation. For example, says Thigpen, a large paper company recently agreed to give TNC agricultural and environmental easements on property the paper company owns near Richmond, Virginia, on which stands the oldest working farm in America. As with a land donation, the farmer or landowner who agrees to the easement gets some kind of tax break. Often, they like the idea of doing something for the environment as well, says Thigpen.

How does the land trust decide what land or water it wants to try to save? That varies widely. Sometimes, it's a matter of wanting to make sure there's park area in a new residential development. Sometimes the issues are larger. TNC, for example, emphasizes acquiring areas where there's a threat to a natural community. This may involve endangered species, but TNC also thinks in terms of "rare" and "relatively rare" species, and of the uniqueness of the land—saving areas representing the best of their kind, such as the best oak hardwood forests, for example. Databases help keep track of such efforts.

"It's the best job in the nature conservancy field," says Basset of acquisitions work. "Those of us who have done it have dreams about going back. Why? It's very exciting, for one thing. But it's also very tangible. You can see the results of what you've done. And those results are very long-lasting."

Requirements

High School

Many courses available to high school students can serve as a good preparation for a career as a land acquisition professional. Science courses from biology to ecology will help you understand the technical aspects of environmental concerns and appreciate the lands you'll be working with.

Communications courses, such as English and speech, will help you negotiate with landowners, while business and math classes will prepare you for work with contracts and tax documents.

Postsecondary Training

Good negotiating and deal-making skills are more important to an acquisitions professional than any specific schooling or work background, according to Basset. For example, he says, one of TNC's best land acquisitions people was a philosophy major and ran hospitals before getting into land acquisitions.

"There's no place to go to school to become a land trust director" or land acquisitions professional, agrees Roe. "It's still so new; it's wide open." Land trust and preserve work in general draws people from all kinds of career areas, from city planning and land-use consulting to law and journalism. Real estate backgrounds are especially useful for people wishing to concentrate on the acquisitions side of land trust work.

Other Requirements

"Communication skills are very important," he says. "People who are very smart, can think on their feet, have two or three alternative scenarios in mind when they meet to negotiate, have all the facts in mind. It's something that's hard to measure in an interview. We say we look for an insurance salesperson with soul."

Exploring

To explore a career with land trusts, check your local library for land trust publications like the Land Trust Alliance's book *Starting a Land Trust*. You can also try contacting the large national land trust organizations for career information. The large national organizations should also be able to provide you with the names of local groups to get involved with.

Starting Out

Volunteering for or doing an internship with a land trust would be an excellent way to enter the field. "Less than half of land trusts have any paid staff," notes Roe. Large statewide organizations are probably the best bets for internships, as are the national organizations. Finally, one option for entering this field is to help start a land trust in your area yourself!

Advancement

Advancement will depend on the size of the land trust organization. A project manager with the Trust for Public Land might move up into an administrative position, for example, or get more complicated cases. Basset became a TNC intern when he was in graduate school, and then rose through the ranks as a chapter director, regional director, and finally director of human resources in TNC's headquarters. Acquisitions work he did along the way was among the most satisfying jobs he's done, he now says. Other options might be to move over to a federal agency that manages federal lands, although these jobs are scarce right now, or into the for-profit sector, such as with a consulting firm or a private company that manages large parcels of land, like a timber company.

Earnings

Again, less than half of the land trusts have paid staff. However, a 1994 survey of the executive directors of land trusts belonging to the Land Trust Alliance revealed a median salary of $33,000. "It varies a lot regionally," notes Roe. Acquisitions people with the big national groups may earn $40,000 or more per year.

Work Environment

This job can take you literally "out in the field," checking out land or water parcels the land trust is considering acquiring; it also can bring you to the negotiating table, where you'll be sitting down with landowners hashing out a deal. Land trusts exist all over the country. Work with a large national organization might involve travel to help out the smaller land trust organizations. Hours, benefits, and other particulars will vary depending on the specific land trust and its resources.

Outlook

The outlook for land trust work currently is brighter than that for federal land and water conservation jobs. Land trusts are "going strong" right now, says Roe, and Basset adds that there seems to be good support for such efforts in Washington, DC, and nationwide. The entire land and water conservation segment, of which land trust and preserve management is a part, is growing at a rate of 1 to 5 percent per year.

For More Information

The following is a national organization of more than 700 land trusts nationwide. Write for an InfoPak of jobs and job descriptions ($20):

Land Trust Alliance
1319 F Street, NW, Suite 501
Washington, DC 20004-1106
Tel: 202-638-4725
Web: http://www.lta.org/

The following specializes in land trusts and land trust management for areas with rare or endangered species. Call 1-800-628-6860 for information about internships with TNC state chapters or at the TNC headquarters:

The Nature Conservancy
1815 Lynn Street
Arlington, VA 22209
Tel: 703-841-5300
Web: http://www.tnc.org

SCA's monthly publication Earth Work *includes job listings.*

Student Conservation Association
PO Box 550
Charlestown, NH 03603
Tel: 603-543-1700
Web: http://www.sca-inc.org/

The Trust for Public Land (TPL)
116 New Montgomery Street, Fourth Floor
San Francisco, CA 94105
Tel: 415-447-4543

Land Trust or Preserve Managers

Biology Earth science	School Subjects
Communication/ideas Leadership/management	Personal Skills
Primarily outdoors One location with some travel	Work Environment
Master's degree	Minimum Education Level
$12,000 to $27,000 to $60,000	Salary Range
None available	Certification or Licensing
Faster than the average	Outlook

Overview

Land trust or preserve managers are part of private and federal efforts to pre-serve land or water from development; subdivision; pollution; overly heavy recreational, grazing, agricultural, or other use; or other human action. The management tasks of land trusts or preserves vary widely, from monitoring the site, inventorying species, or managing natural resources to specialized conservation and preservation work. Examples of the latter might include doing controlled burnings, re-creating lost or damaged ecosystems, and restoring native plants and animals.

History

Efforts to conserve land and water go back more than one hundred years in this country and have been driven by two key forces: the government and private citizens' or community groups. Alarm about diminishing wilderness areas in the West led to the establishment of the first national parks and preserves by our government in the late 19th century. Around that time, the government also set aside four Civil War battlefields as national battlefield parks, the first historic sites so acquired by the United States government.

The single most influential figure in early conservation efforts was Theodore Roosevelt, the 26th president of the United States. Roosevelt fell in love with the West as a young man, when ill health led him there to seek better air. He owned a ranch in the Dakota Territory and wrote many books about his experiences in the West.

When he became president in 1901, Roosevelt used the position to help preserve his beloved West. He and his administrators pushed conservation as part of an overall strategy for the responsible use of natural resources, including forests, pastures, fish, game, soil, and minerals. This both increased public awareness of and support for conservation and led to important early conservation legislation. Roosevelt's administration especially emphasized the preservation of forests, wildlife, park lands, wilderness areas, and watershed areas and carried out such work as the first inventory of natural resources in this country.

Theodore Roosevelt was, rightfully, very proud of the monumental accomplishments of his administration in conserving the natural resources of the nation. He wrote, "During the seven and one-half years closing on March 4, 1909 (the years of his administration), more was accomplished for the protection of wildlife in the United States than during all the previous years, excepting only the creation of Yellowstone National Park."

But government action is only part of this story. Individual citizens forming private nonprofit land trusts, plus national nonprofit land trust organizations, have saved countless acres of land and water as well. They, too, have their roots in the last century.

Back in 1891, the city of Boston was bursting at the seams. A thriving shipbuilding industry plus other commercial and industrial pursuits had helped that city boom in the 19th century. Boston also had seen an explosion in immigrant population, particularly Irish immigrants. The Captains of Industry and their families poured money into the arts, helping Boston gain a reputation as the "Athens of America."

Some Bostonians, however, were troubled by the rapid development that swallowed up areas at the edges of the city. They were concerned that remaining wild areas were going to disappear and that many people living in the city were never going to have access to open lands and wild areas.

One group of citizens took action. They formed a group called the Trustees of Reservations, bought up some of the undeveloped land themselves, and opened the areas to the public for recreational use. This was the first official land trust in the country, and it paved the way for a whole movement of private land trusts.

Land trusts have been started by single individuals as well as large groups; they have worked to protect just a few acres of land up to hundreds of acres, depending on the part of the country and the trust's resources. Sometimes trusts just acquire the land or easements on it; but sometimes, and increasingly in recent years, they also take steps to environmentally manage it.

Land trusts saw "gigantic growth" in the mid- to late-1980s, says Kieran Roe, information specialist for the Land Trust Alliance (LTA), the largest national organization of land trusts. Following a slight dip in the early 1990s due to the recession, they are going strong today. Reports of the exact number of land trusts in this country vary; Roe says The Land Trust Alliance is aware of about 1,100, of which 700 are members of the LTA.

Sometimes land trusts work in cooperation with U.S. federal agencies for managing lands. This is true of The Nature Conservancy (TNC), for example, a very large national land trust organization specializing in rare wildlife and habitats. "A number of things of rarity on this planet occur on public land," explains Chuck Basset, vice president of human resources for TNC. "We can help manage it, give advice, and counsel on it."

Consulting firms specializing in land trust or preserve management also exist and may be called in to help with special areas like ecosystem restoration or forestry management. Finally, some private corporations, such as utility companies or timber companies, own and manage large parcels of land; their land management may include conservation and preservation of areas such as forest wetlands.

The Job

Land trusts acquire land by buying it, getting the landowner to donate it, arranging for easements on it, or purchasing the development rights to it. Land acquisition may be just one of many tasks of a land trust employee, such as the executive director; or in larger land trusts, it may be the sole job of one or more land acquisition professionals.

What is involved with managing a land trust or preserve? That depends on the specific land or water involved and its needs, who's doing the managing, how much funding and staffing is available, and other factors. "There are many land trusts out there, so there's a wide range of things that might happen," says Roe. That's true for land and water managed by federal agencies, too.

Staffing of land trusts can be minimal, particularly in the early years of the trust. "At first it might just be one person, an executive director, who does everything from handling correspondence to walking the land," says Roe. "If the land trust grows larger, it may add more people who can then focus on specific tasks, including management of the land." A few land trusts, particularly some of the large statewide land trusts, are large enough to have a staff of 30 paid people or more.

As for federally managed lands, these, too, can have varying levels of staffing and funding that affect what specific work is done. But the federal government employs about 75 percent of all people working in land and water conservation, and in general the federal agencies have greater resources than private land trusts. For example, all national parks have natural resource management departments that carry out tasks from ensuring environmental compliance to specialized conservation/preservation work.

Specific work varies in different parts of the country, from forests to the Everglades to coastal areas, and ranges from simply monitoring the land to doing specialized work like re-creating destroyed ecosystems. Examples include:

Planning for better use of land and water. If the land is a recreational area, for example, managers might plan how to prevent over-use.

Species inventory. Cataloging plant and animal species helps establish the "baseline" needed to plan for the area, explains Basset of TNC. "Our business is biodiversity conservation," he says. "So when we acquire land, we want to check the diversity there—species diversity, health of species, age of species. We hire contract or seasonal workers to do this; then stewardship scientists set up the plan."

Restoration or re-creation of damaged or destroyed ecosystems. Getting an area back to how it used to be may involve cleaning up pollution, bringing back native species, and getting rid of non-native species. Landscape architects, biologists, botanists, *ecologists,* and others may help do such work. Restoration of wetlands, one example of this work, including forest wetlands, may involve wetlands ecologists, fish and wildlife scientists, and botanists.

Habitat protection. Protecting wildlife habitats, particularly those of rare or endangered species, is another important task. At least 600 plants and animals in the United States alone currently are endangered, according to the U.S. Fish and Wildlife Service.

Prescribed burnings. Management of prairies, forests, or rangelands may involve controlled burnings. After the fire, specialists may go in and inventory species. Pitch pine communities in New York and New Jersey, and longleaf pine forests in Virginia, Texas, and other parts of the South, are just some areas handled this way, according to Basset.

Rangeland management. In addition to prescribed burnings, this may involve controlled grazing by bison or cattle to keep plant life under control.

Requirements

High School

Recommended high school course work for those interested in scientific work includes biology, chemistry, and physics as well as botany and ecology. All potential land trust or preserve managers can benefit from courses in business, computer science, English, and speech.

Postsecondary Training

At the undergraduate level, students might get a natural science degree, such as zoology, biology, or botany. Chipley says there's also been growing interest in degrees in conservation biology, which focuses on the conservation of specific plant and animal communities, from schools such as the University of Wisconsin-Madison. Another key school is the forestry school at Yale. Land and water conservation is a popular field, so those interested in the natural science areas are advised to earn at least a master's degree.

Other Requirements

Because land trusts tend to be entrepreneurial, they need people skilled in business administration, finance, and law to run the financial end of the trust, raise funds, negotiate deals, and handle tax matters. Communications professionals are needed to get the word out about the trusts' work.

Exploring

There are many ways to explore a career in land and water conservation. Read up on land and water conservation in the library, contact nonprofit land trusts or federal agencies for information about current projects, or check out the degree programs at local universities. The Internet is another rich source of up-to-date information; some sites are listed at the end of this article.

Employers

The federal government, in its various agencies and branches, is the largest employer of land trust professionals. State and local government agencies also employ some land trust professionals in a variety of positions. Outside of government, potential employers include numerous nonprofit organizations and private land trusts. Additionally, large banks and other similar institutions employ land trust specialists.

Starting Out

This field is so popular that many people get their start in less traditional ways, such as contract or seasonal work, volunteer work, and internships.

Even people graduating with a master's degree may only be able to land contract work at first, according to the Environmental Careers Organization (ECO). Contract work is work done on a per-project or freelance basis: you sign on for one specific project and move on when it's done. Contract workers usually are specialists, such as ecologists or botanists, according to Basset.

The need for them is high in the summer months when biological inventorying work is plentiful.

Volunteer and internship opportunities are available at many environmental organizations. These opportunities frequently lead to paid positions and always provide valuable experience.

Advancement

There are three general advancement paths for land trust professionals. The traditional promotion path might begin with an internship, then progress to positions of increasing power and responsibility. The second path involves expansion of duties within a specialty field. For example, someone who starts out as a land protection specialist in North Carolina may not have any desire to move out of that work; therefore, his or her job may be expanded laterally—broadening into consulting work in the specialty in other parts of the state, or even nationwide. Third, a person may opt for a "demotion"—getting back to land protection and conservation fieldwork, for example, after having served in an administrative position.

Earnings

The salary range for land and water conservation professionals is about $12,000 to $18,000 for entry-level jobs, to an average $27,000 to $34,000, up to $50,000 to $60,000 for a master's and experience. Jobs with private companies tend to start out closer to $25,000 and average about $35,000, according to ECO. Federal government agency jobs pay more than state or local government jobs. Nonprofit groups' salaries can be competitive but tend to be at the lower end of the pay range. Salaries also tend to vary by region.

Work Environment

Tromping around in the wilderness, inventorying plant and animal species, working outdoors to help develop a natural area—all of these are possible if you work in land or water conservation, particularly if you're working as a natural scientist or in support of the scientists. Administrators, communicators, lawyers, and others more often will find themselves in offices, of course, especially when they're working for larger organizations. If you like the idea of working outdoors, you're not alone: ECO says people in land and water conservation tend to stay in their jobs longer than people in other environmental careers, attesting to the appeal of these jobs.

Outlook

Right now, the best opportunities appear to be with the private land trusts and national land trust organizations, as opposed to the federal agencies. With little exception, none of the federal agencies is expected to see big growth over the next few years. On the other hand, following the slight slow-down of the early 1990s, the private land trusts are growing right now.

For More Information

The following is a national organization of more than seven hundred land trusts nationwide. Write for an InfoPak of jobs and job descriptions ($20):

Land Trust Alliance
1319 F Street, NW, Suite 501
Washington, DC 20004-1106
Tel: 202-638-4725
Web: http://www.lta.org/

This conservation organization offers fellowships for graduate work in conservation, places people in paid internships, and more:

National Wildlife Federation
1400 16th Street, NW
Washington, DC 20036
Tel: 202-797-6800
Web: http://www.nwf.org

The following organization specializes in land trusts and land trust management for areas with rare or endangered species. Call 1-800-628-6860 for information about internships with TNC state chapters or at the TNC headquarters:

The Nature Conservancy
1815 Lynn Street
Arlington, VA 22209
Tel: 703-841-5300
Web: http://www.tnc.org

SCA's monthly publication Earth Work *includes job listings. Also contact this group for information regarding volunteer positions in natural resource management, including with federal land management agencies:*

Student Conservation Association
PO Box 550
Charlestown, NH 03603
Tel: 603-543-1700
Web: http://www.sca-inc.org

Marine Biologists

Biology Earth science	School Subjects
Mechanical/manipulative Technical/scientific	Personal Skills
Indoors and outdoors Primarily multiple locations	Work Environment
Bachelor's degree	Minimum Education Level
$21,000 to $36,000 to $100,000+	Salary Range
Required for certain positions	Certification or Licensing
About as fast as the average	Outlook

Overview

Marine biologists study species of plants and animals that live in saltwater, their interactions with one another, and how they influence and are influenced by environmental factors. Marine biology is a branch of science, and biologists in this area work in myriad industries—government agencies, universities, aquaria, and fish hatcheries, to name a few. They generally work either in a laboratory setting or in the field, which in this case means being in or on the ocean or its margins.

History

Marine biologists started to make their study into a real science around the 19th century with a series of British expeditions. In 1872, the HMS *Challenger* set sail with such scientists as Sir Charles Wyville Thomson and Sir John Murray on the most important oceanographic mission of all time. Over four years, they traveled 69,000 miles and cataloged 4,717 new species of marine plants and animals. Many marine scientists view the reports from this expedition as the basis of modern oceanography.

Before that time, marine scientists believed that sea creatures inhabited only shallow waters. They believed that the intense cold, pressure, and darkness below about 1,800 feet could not support life. Then, in the late 1860s, the HMS *Lightning* and the HMS *Porcupine* made hauls from below 14,400 feet that contained bizarre new creatures.

Scientists began to build precision equipment for measuring oceanic conditions. Among these were thermometers that could gauge the temperature at any depth, containers that could be closed at a desired depth to collect seawater, and coring instruments that could sample bottom sediments. Scientists also figured out techniques for measuring levels of salt, oxygen, and nutrients right on board ship.

20th-century innovations such as underwater cameras, oxygen tanks, submersible craft, and heavy-duty diving gear that can withstand extremes of cold and pressure have made it possible for biologists to observe sea creatures in their natural habitats.

The Job

Marine biologists study and work with sea creatures in their natural environment—the oceans of the world and tidal pools along shorelines—as well as in laboratories. These scientists are interested in knowing how the ocean's changing conditions, such as temperature and chemical pollutants, can affect the plants and animals that live there. For example, what happens when certain species become extinct or are no longer safe to be eaten? Marine biologists can begin to understand how the world's food supply is diminished and help come up with solutions that can change such problem situations.

The work of these scientists is also important for improving and controlling sport and commercial fishing. Through underwater exploration, marine biologists have discovered that the world's coral reefs are being damaged by humans; they have also charted the migration of whales and counted the decreasing numbers of certain species; they have observed dolphins being accidentally caught in tuna fishermen's nets. By writing reports and research papers about such discoveries, a marine biologist can inform others about problems that need attention and begin to make important changes that could help the world.

To study plants and animals, marine biologists spend some of their work time in the ocean wearing wet suits to keep warm (because of the frigid temperature below the surface of the sea) and scuba gear to breathe underwater.

They gather specimens with a slurp gun, which sucks fish into a specimen bag without causing them injury. They must learn how to conduct their research without damaging the marine environment, which is delicate. Marine biologists must also face the threat to their own safety from dangerous fish and underwater conditions.

Marine biologists also study life in tidal pools along the shoreline. They might collect specimens at the same time of day for days at a time. They would keep samples from different pools separate and keep records of the pool's location and the types and measurements of the specimens taken. This ensures that the studies are as accurate as possible. After collecting specimens, they keep them in a portable aquarium tank on board ship. After returning to land, which may not be for weeks or months, marine biologists begin to study specimens in a laboratory, often with other people working on the same study. They might, for example, check the amount of oxygen in a sea turtle's bloodstream to learn how the turtles can stay underwater for so long; or measure the "antifreeze" in the blood of an arctic fish to discover how it can survive frigid temperatures.

Requirements

High School

High school students should take biology and other sciences such as chemistry, earth sciences, and computer science. Participation in science clubs will give you experience working on projects with a team.

Postsecondary Training

If you're interested in marine biology you should take basic science courses such as biology, botany, and chemistry. However, classes don't end there. For instance, in biology you might be required to choose from marine invertebrate biology, ecology, oceanography, genetics, animal physiology, plant physiology, and aquatic plant biology. You might also be required to choose several more specific classes such as ichthyology, vertebrate structure, population biology, developmental biology, biology of microorganisms, evolution, and cell biology. Classes in other subjects will also be required, like computer science, math (including algebra, trigonometry, calculus, analytical geometry, and statistics), and physics.

Although it is possible to get a job as a marine biologist with just a bachelor's degree, most marine biologists have a master's or doctoral degree.

Certification or Licensing

If you are going to be diving, organizations like the Professional Association of Diving Instructors (PADI) provide basic certification. Training for scientific diving is more in-depth and requires passing an exam. It is also critical that divers learn cardiopulmonary resuscitation (CPR) and first aid. Also, if you'll be handling hazardous materials, such as formaldehyde, strong acids, or radioactive nucleotides, you must be licensed.

Other Requirements

You should have an ability to ask questions and solve problems, observe small details carefully, do research, and analyze mathematical information. You should be inquisitive and must think for yourself. This is essential to the scientific method. You must use your creative ability and be inventive in order to design experiments; these are the scientist's means of asking questions of the natural world. Working in the field often requires some strength and physical endurance, particularly if you are scuba diving or if you are doing fieldwork in tidepools, which can involve hiking over miles of shore at low tide, keeping your footing on weedy rocks, and lifting and turning stones to find specimens.

Exploring

Volunteering at a local aquarium is an excellent way to learn about marine life and about the life of a marine biologist.

You can begin diving training while in high school. Between the ages of 12 and 15 you can earn a Junior Open Water Diver certification, which allows you to dive in the company of a certified adult. When you turn 15, you can upgrade your certification to Open Water Diver.

Employers

Employers in this field range from pharmaceutical companies researching marine sources for medicines to federal agencies that regulate marine fisheries, such as the fisheries division of the National Oceanographic and Atmospheric Association (NOAA). Aquariums hire marine biologists to collect and study specimens.

After acquiring many years of experience, you might be eligible for a faculty position at a school like the Scripps Institute of Oceanography or the University of Washington.

Marine products companies, such as Federal Marine Colloids, which manufactures carrageenan and agar (extracted from algae and used as thickening agents in foods), hire biologists to design and carry out research.

Jobs in marine biology are based mostly in coastal areas, though some biologists work inland as university professors, or perhaps as *paleontologists* who search for and study marine fossils.

Starting Out

With only a bachelor's degree, you may be able to get a job as a laboratory technician in a state or federal agency. Some aquaria will hire you straight out of college, but generally it's easier to get a paid position if you've worked as a volunteer at the aquarium. You'll need a more advanced degree to get into more technical positions such as consulting, writing for scientific journals, or conducting research.

Web sites are good resources for employment information. If you can find the human resources section of an aquarium's home page, it will tell you whom to contact to find out about openings and may even provide job listings. Federal agencies may also have Web sites with human resource information.

Professors who know you as a student might be able to help you locate a position as they might have connections in the professional world.

Another good way to make contacts is by attending conferences or seminars sponsored by aquatic science organizations such as the American Society of Limnology and Oceanography or the Mid-Atlantic Marine Education Association.

Advancement

If you are a lab technician with a four-year degree, you may become a senior lab tech after years with the same lab. Generally, though, taking on greater responsibility or getting into more technical work means further education. If you want to do research in any setting, you'll need a graduate degree or at least to be working on one. To get an administrative position with a marine products company or a faculty position at a university, you'll need at least a master's degree, and if you hope to become a senior scientist at a marine station or a full professor, you must have a doctoral degree.

Earnings

Salaries will vary quite a lot depending on level of education, type of work, size and location of the operation, and level of experience. Based on information from the American Society of Limnology and Oceanography, those with bachelor's degrees and no experience might find work with the federal government with a salary around $21,000 to $33,000. The average biologist earns about $36,000 yearly. However, those with doctoral degrees in marine biology or one of its subfields can earn as much as $80,000. Senior scientists and full professors at universities can make more than $100,000.

Work Environment

Most marine biologists don't actually spend a lot of time diving. However, researchers might spend a couple of hours periodically breathing from a scuba tank below some waters, like Monterey Bay or the Gulf of Maine. They might gather samples from the deck of a large research vessel during a two-month expedition, or they might be sitting in a conference room with several other research biologists.

In most marine biology work, some portion of time is spent in the lab analyzing samples of seawater or collating data on a computer. Many hours are spent in solitude reading papers in scientific journals or writing papers for publication.

Instructors or professors work in classrooms interacting with students and directing student lab work.

Those who work for an aquarium, as consultants for private corporations, or in universities work an average of 40 to 50 hours a week.

Outlook

Generally speaking, there are more marine biologists than there are paying positions at present. Changes in the earth's environment, such as global warming and increased levels of heavy metals in the global water cycle, will most likely prompt more research and result in slightly more jobs in different subfields.

Greater need for smart management of the world's fisheries, research by pharmaceutical companies into deriving medicines from marine organisms, and cultivation of marine food alternatives such as seaweeds and plankton are other factors that may increase the demand for marine biologists in the near future.

For More Information

For information on careers, contact:

American Society of Limnology and Oceanography
Web: http://www.aslo.org

This center for research and education in global science currently runs more than 300 research programs and uses a fleet of four ships to conduct expeditions over the entire globe.

Scripps Institution of Oceanography
University of California, San Diego
8602 La Jolla Shores Drive
La Jolla, CA 92037-1508
Tel: 619-534-3624
Email: siocomm@sio.ucsd.edu
Web: http://www-sio.ucsd.edu/

Meteorologists

	School Subjects
Geography Physics	
	Personal Skills
Helping/teaching Technical/scientific	
	Work Environment
Primarily indoors Primarily one location	
	Minimum Education Level
Bachelor's degree	
	Salary Range
$19,500 to $57,000 to $100,000+	
	Certification or Licensing
Recommended	
	Outlook
Little change or more slowly than the average	

Overview

Meteorologists study weather conditions and forecast weather changes. By analyzing weather maps covering large geographic areas and related charts, like upper-air maps and soundings, they can predict the movement of fronts, precipitation, and pressure areas. They forecast such data as temperature, winds, precipitation, cloud cover, and flying conditions. To predict future weather patterns and to develop increased accuracy in weather study and forecasting, meteorologists conduct research on such subjects as atmospheric electricity, clouds, precipitation, hurricanes, and data collected from weather satellites. Other areas of research used to forecast weather may include ocean currents and temperature.

History

Meteorology is an observational science, the study of the atmosphere, weather, and climate. The basic meteorological instruments were all invented hundreds of years ago. Galileo (1564-1642) invented the thermometer in 1593, and Evangelista Torricelli (1608-47) invented the barometer in 1643. Simultaneous comparison and study of weather was impossible until the telegraph was invented. Observations of the upper atmosphere from balloons and airplanes started after World War I. Not until World War II, however, was great financial support given to the development of meteorology. In the war, a very clear-cut relationship was established between the effectiveness of new weapons and the atmosphere.

More accurate instruments for measuring and observing weather conditions, new systems of communication, and the development of satellites, radar, and high-speed computers to process and analyze weather data have helped meteorologists and the general public acquire a better understanding of the atmosphere.

The Job

Although most people think of weather forecasting when they think of meteorology, meteorologists do many other kinds of work also. They perform research on subjects ranging from radioactive fallout to the dynamics of hurricanes. They study the ozone levels in the stratosphere. Some teach in colleges and universities.

Many meteorologists are needed in radio and televised weather forecasting programs. Networks usually hire their own staff of meteorologists.

Meteorologists generally specialize in one branch of this rapidly developing science; however, the lines of specialization are not clearly drawn and meteorologists often work in more than one area of specialization. The largest group of specialists are called *operational meteorologists,* the technical name for weather forecasters. They interpret current weather information, such as air pressure, temperature, humidity, and wind velocity, reported by observers, weather satellites, weather radar, and remote sensors in many parts of the world. They use this data to make short- and long-range forecasts for given regions. Operational meteorologists also use Doppler radar, which detects rotational patterns in violent thunderstorms, in order to better predict tornadoes, thunderstorms, and flash floods as well as their direction and intensity. Other specialists include *climatologists* who study past records to discover weather patterns for a given region. The climatologist compiles, makes statistical analyses of, and interprets data on temperature, sunlight, rainfall, humidity, and wind for a particular area over a long period of time. Such data is used in weather forecasting, aviation, agriculture, commerce, and public health.

Dynamic meteorologists study the physical laws related to air currents. *Physical meteorologists* study the physical nature of the atmosphere, including its chemical composition and electrical, acoustical, and optical properties. They aid in studies of environmental problems such as air pollution, global warming, and ozone depletion. *Industrial meteorologists* work in a variety of private industries, focusing their expertise on such problems as smoke control and air pollution.

The tools used by meteorologists include weather balloons, instrumented aircraft's, radar, satellites, and computers.

Instrumented aircraft are high-performance airplanes used to observe many kinds of weather. Radar is used to detect rain or snow, as well as other weather. Doppler radar can measure wind speed and direction. It has become the best tool for predicting severe weather.

Satellites use advanced remote sensing to measure temperature, wind, and other characteristics of the atmosphere at many levels. The entire surface of the earth can be observed with satellites.

The introduction of computers has changed research and forecasting of weather. The fastest computers are used in atmospheric research, as well as large scale weather forecasting. Computers are used to produce simulations of upcoming weather.

Requirements

High School

You can best prepare for a college major in meteorology by taking high school course work in mathematics, geography, computer science, physics, and chemistry. A good command of English is essential, because you must be able to describe complex weather events and patterns in a clear and concise way.

Postsecondary Training

Although some beginners in meteorological work have majored in subjects related to meteorology, the normal minimal requirement for work in this field is a bachelor's degree in meteorology from one of the almost 100 colleges offering a major in this field. The federal government, for example, requires beginners to have a minimum of 20 semester hours in meteorology (including six hours in dynamic meteorology and six hours in weather analysis and forecasting) supplemented by work in physics and differential and integral calculus. Advanced graduate training in meteorology and related areas is required for research and teaching positions as well as for other high-level positions in meteorology. Doctorates are quite common among high-level personnel.

Because the armed forces require the services of so many meteorologists, they have programs to send recently commissioned, new college graduates to civilian universities for intensive work in meteorology.

Certification or Licensing

The American Meteorological Society provides certification of consulting meteorologists and awards a seal of approval to recognize competence in radio and television weather forecasting.

Other Requirements

Meteorologists must be able to work well under pressure in order to meet deadlines or plot severe weather systems. They must be able to communicate complex theories and events, aloud and in writing. They must be able to absorb pertinent information quickly and pass it on to co-workers and the public in a clear, calm manner. Meteorologists who work in broadcasting must have especially good communication skills in order to deal with the pressure and deadlines of the newsroom.

Exploring

Students who are interested in meteorology can explore career possibilities in several ways. Each year the federal government's National Weather Service accepts a limited number of student volunteers, mostly college students but also a few high school students. Some universities offer credit for a college student's volunteer work in connection with meteorology courses. The National Oceanographic and Atmospheric Administration has details about the volunteer program. The armed forces can also be a means of gaining experience in meteorology.

Interviews can be held with meteorologists at airports or at colleges and universities offering work in meteorology. Students can also gain more information by getting in touch with the sources listed at the end of this article.

Employers

The largest employer of meteorologists is the federal government. Most hold civilian positions, although many opportunities are available in the armed forces. There are also opportunities for meteorologists in educational settings. There are hundreds of meteorologists teaching at institutions of higher education.

There are about 10,000 meteorologists employed in the United States. In addition, meteorological faculties in colleges and universities account for another 1,000 or so jobs in this field. The National Oceanic and Atmospheric Administration (NOAA) employs about 2,700 meteorologists. About two-thirds of the NOAA meteorologists work in the National Weather Service; the rest work mainly in research. The Department of Defense employs more than 280 civilian meteorologists.

Most civilian meteorologists work for private industry, including weather consulting firms, engineering service firms, commercial airlines, radio and television stations, and companies that design and manufacture meteorological instruments and aircraft and missiles. Others, not classified officially as meteorologists, teach meteorology in colleges and universities.

In addition to the civilian meteorologists, thousands of members of the armed forces also engage in government meteorological work.

Starting Out

Individuals may enter the field of meteorology in a number of ways. Some are assisted in securing positions by placement officials at the colleges and universities where they have studied. Others, who have volunteered at the National Weather Service, may receive permanent positions as meteorologists upon completing their formal training. Members of the armed forces who have done work in meteorology often assume positions in meteorology when they return to civilian life. In fact, the armed forces give preference in the employment of civilian meteorologists to former military personnel with appropriate experience. Individuals interested in teaching and research careers generally assume these positions upon receiving their doctorates in meteorology or related subjects.

Other federal employers of meteorologists include the Department of Defense, the National Aeronautics and Space Administration (NASA), and the Department of Agriculture.

Advancement

Meteorologists employed by the National Weather Service advance according to civil service regulations. After meeting certain experiential and educational requirements, they advance to classifications that carry more pay and, often, more responsibility. Opportunities available to meteorologists employed by airlines are more limited. A few of these workers, however, do advance to such positions as flight dispatcher and to administrative and supervisory positions. A few meteorologists go into business for themselves by establishing their own weather-consulting services. Meteorologists who are employed in teaching and research in colleges and universities receive advancement by being promoted in academic rank or by assuming administrative positions in the university setting.

Earnings

Beginning salaries of meteorologists are related to the amount of formal training they have received and the setting in which they are employed. The average salary of meteorologists employed by the federal government is about $50,500 a year. Starting salaries for government meteorologists with a bachelor's degree range from $19,500 to $24,200; with a master's degree, $24,200 to $29,600; and with a doctoral degree, $35,800 to $42,900—with the higher salaries for each degree being awarded to those with the highest grades.

In broadcast meteorology, salaries vary greatly. Typical starting salaries begin at $20,000 a year. Experienced meteorologists average $46,000 per year. In large media markets, a small percentage of broadcast meteorologists can earn over $100,000 a year.

Work Environment

Weather stations are operated on a 24-hour, 7-day-a-week basis. This means that some meteorologists, often on a rotating basis, work evenings and weekends. Although most of these weather stations are at airports located near cities, a number of weather stations are located in isolated and remote areas. One of the most remote meteorological posts is on the Antarctic. However, it provides much of the most interesting and relevant data in meteorology. In such places, the life of a meteorologist can be quiet and lonely. Operational meteorologists often work overtime during weather emergencies such as hurricanes. Meteorologists who work in college and university settings enjoy the same working conditions as do other professors.

For More Information

The following organization offers a newsletter, journals, employment announcements, scholarships and student information.

American Meteorological Society
45 Beacon Street
Boston, MA 02108
Tel: 617-227-2425
Email: amsmem@ametsoc
Web: http://www.ametsoc.org

For job announcements, a newsletter, and science links, contact:

National Weather Association
6704 Wolke Court
Montgomery, AL 36116-2134
Tel: 334-213-0388

Oceanographers

School Subjects
- Biology
- Chemistry

Personal Skills
- Communication/ideas
- Technical/scientific

Work Environment
- Indoors and outdoors
- One location with some travel

Minimum Education Level
- Bachelor's degree

Salary Range
- $21,000 to $45,500 to $84,800

Certification or Licensing
- None available

Outlook
- Little change or more slowly than the average

Overview

Oceanographers obtain information about the ocean through observations, surveys, and experiments. They study the physical, chemical, and biological composition of the ocean and the geological structure of the seabed. They also analyze phenomena involving the water itself, the atmosphere above it, the land beneath it, and the coastal borders. They study acoustical properties of water so that a comprehensive and unified picture of the ocean's behavior may be developed. A *limnologist* is a specialist who studies fresh water life.

History

The oceans hold some 97 percent of the water on Earth and cover more than two-thirds of its surface. Oceans hold food, chemicals, and minerals, yet oceanography is a fairly new science. In fact, according to the Oceanography Society, it has only been during the 21st century that we have gotten the first "global glimpse" of how the oceans work. With such inventions as deep-sea diving gear, scuba, and the bathysphere (a steel diving sphere for deep-sea observation), scientists are undertaking more detailed studies of underwater life. Oceanography includes studying air and sea interaction in weather forecasting, solving sea mining problems, predicting and preventing pollution, studying sea life, and improving methods of deriving foods from the ocean. Perhaps because oceanography is a fairly new field, most universities do not offer graduate degrees in it specifically. That is why many oceanographers are trained as physicists, chemists, geologists, and biologists who then apply their expertise to studying the ocean.

The Job

Oceanographers collect and study data about the motions of ocean water (waves, currents, and tides), marine life (sea plants and animals and their habits), ore and petroleum deposits (minerals and oils contained in the nodules and oozes of the ocean floor), and the contour of the ocean floor (ocean mountains, valleys, and depths). Many of their findings are compiled for maps, charts, graphs, and special reports and manuals.

Oceanographers may spend some of their time on the water each year gathering data and making observations. Additional oceanographic work is done on dry land by people who infrequently go to sea. Experiments using models or captive organisms may be conducted in the seaside laboratory.

Oceanographers use equipment designed and manufactured in special shops. This equipment includes devices to measure depths by sound impulses, special thermometers to measure water temperatures, special cameras for underwater photography, and diving gear and machines like the bathyscaphe—a submersible ship for deep-sea exploration. In addition to such commonly used equipment, many new devices have been developed for specific types of underwater work. The oceanographer of the future may be using such tools as a hydraulic miner (a dredge to extract nodules from the ocean floor), an electronic beater (a machine used to drive fish), dye curtains, fish pumps, and instrument buoys. New technologies being developed today include satellite sensors and acoustic current measuring devices.

The oceanographer is usually part of a highly skilled team, with each member specializing in one of the four main branches of the profession. In actual work, however, there is a tremendous amount of overlap among the four branches. *Biological oceanographers* or *marine biologists* study all aspects of the ocean's plant and animal life. They are interested in how the life develops and interacts with and adapts to its environment. *Physical oceanographers* study such physical aspects of the ocean as temperature and density, waves and currents, and the relationship between the ocean and the atmosphere. *Geological oceanographers* study the topographic features and physical composition of the ocean bottom. Their work greatly contributes to our knowledge and understanding of Earth's history. *Chemical oceanographers* and *marine geochemists* investigate the chemical composition of the water and ocean floor. They may study seawater components, pollutants, and trace chemicals, which are small amounts of dissolved substances that give an area of water a certain quality.

Oceanography jobs can be found all over the United States, and not just where the water meets the shore. Although the majority of jobs are on the Pacific, Atlantic, and Gulf coasts, many other jobs are available to the marine scientist. Universities and colleges, and federal and state agencies are the largest employers of oceanographers. But international organizations, private companies, consulting firms, nonprofit laboratories, and local governments also hire them. Sometimes, they are self-employed as consultants with their own businesses.

It is difficult to project what oceanographers of the future may be doing. They may be living and working on the ocean floor. The U.S. Navy Medical Research Laboratory has conducted experiments with people living under 200 feet of water.

Requirements

High School

Because a college degree is required for beginning positions in oceanography, in high school you should take four years of college preparatory courses in science and mathematics. English, writing, and computer classes are also important.

Postsecondary Training

In college, a broad program covering the basic sciences with a major in physics, chemistry, biology, or geology is desirable. In addition, you should include courses in field research or laboratory work in oceanography where available. Graduate work in oceanography is required for most positions in research and teaching. More than 100 institutions offer programs in marine studies, but only 19 universities have graduate programs leading to a doctoral degree in oceanography.

As a college student preparing for graduate work in oceanography, you should take mathematics through differential and integral calculus and at least one year each of chemistry and physics, biology or geology, and a modern foreign language.

Other Requirements

Personal traits helpful to a career in oceanography are a strong interest in science, particularly the physical and earth sciences; an interest in situations involving activities of an abstract and creative nature (observing nature, performing experiments, creating objects); an interest in outdoor activities such as hunting, fishing, swimming, boating, or animal care; an interest in scholarly activities (reading, researching, writing); and other interests that cut across the traditional academic boundaries of biology, chemistry, and physics.

You should have above-average aptitudes in verbal, numerical, and spatial reasoning. Prospective oceanographers should also be able to discriminate detail among objects in terms of their shape, size, color, or markings.

Exploring

Obviously, if you live near coastal regions, you will have an easier time becoming familiar with oceans and ocean life than if you are land-locked. However, some institutions may offer work or leisure-time experiences that will provide participants with opportunities to explore particular aspects of oceanography. Possible opportunities include work in marine or conservation fisheries or on board seagoing vessels, or field experiences in studying rocks, minerals, or aquatic life. If you live or travel near one of the oceanography research centers, such as Woods Hole Oceanographic Institution on Cape Cod, the University of Miami's Institute of Marine Science, or the Scripps Institution of Oceanography in California, you should plan to spend some time learning about their activities and studying their exhibits.

Volunteer work for students is often available with research teams, nonprofit organizations, and public centers such as aquariums. If you do not live near water, try to find summer internships, camps, or programs that involve travel to a coastal area. You can help pave your way into the field by learning all you can about the geology, atmosphere, and plant and animal life of the area where you live, regardless of whether water is present.

Employers

Approximately 50 percent of those working in oceanography and marine-related fields work for federal or state governments. Federal employers of oceanographers, ocean engineers, marine technicians, and those interested in marine policy include the Department of Defense, the Environmental Protection Agency, the U.S. Geological Survey, and the National Biological Survey, among others. State governments often employ oceanographers in environmental agencies or state-funded research projects.

Forty percent of oceanographers are employed by colleges or universities, where they teach, conduct research, write, and consult. The remaining 10 percent of oceanographers work for private industries such as oil companies and nonprofit organizations such as environmental societies. An increasing number of oceanographers are employed each year by industrial firms, particularly those involved in oceanographic instrument and equipment manufacturing, shipbuilding, and chemistry.

Starting Out

Most college placement offices are staffed to help you find positions in business and industry after you graduate. Often positions can be found through friends, relatives, or college professors or through the college's placement office by application and interview. College and university assistantships, instructorships, and professorships are usually obtained by recommendation of your major professor or department chairperson. In addition, internships with the government or private industry during college can often lead to permanent employment after graduation. The American Institute of Biological Sciences maintains an employment service and lists both employers and job seekers.

Advancement

Starting oceanography positions usually involve working as a laboratory or research assistant, with on-the-job training in applying oceanographic principles to the problems at hand. Some beginning oceanographers with Ph.D. degrees may qualify for college teaching or research positions. Experienced personnel, particularly those with advanced graduate work or doctorates, can become supervisors or administrators. Such positions involve considerable responsibility in planning and policymaking or policy interpretation. Those who achieve top-level oceanographer positions may plan and supervise research projects involving a number of workers, or they may be in charge of an oceanographic laboratory or aquarium.

Earnings

While marine scientists are richly rewarded in nonmaterial ways for their diverse and exciting work with the sea, they almost never become wealthy by American standards. Salaries depend on education, experience, and chosen discipline. Supply and demand issues, along with where you work also come into play. Some examples of jobs in the marine sciences that presently pay more than the average include physical oceanography, marine technology and engineering, and computer modeling.

According to a 1996 report by the National Association of Colleges and Employers, those graduating with a bachelor's degree in geology and geological sciences were offered an average starting salary of $32,091. In 1995, the average annual salary for experienced oceanographers working in managerial, supervisory, and nonsupervisory positions was $58,980.

Oceanographers who work for the federal government make salaries based on their education and experience. In 1998, those with a bachelor's degree could start out at the GS-5 level making $21,421 (in the greater Washington, DC-Baltimore metropolitan area). A master's degree lets you qualify for a GS-7 or GS-9 position, which in 1998 paid $26,532 and $32,457, respectively. Beginning oceanographers with a Ph.D. can qualify as a GS-11 or GS-12, making $39,270 or $47,066, respectively, in 1998.

In addition to their regular salaries, oceanographers may supplement their incomes with fees earned from consulting, lecturing, and publishing their findings. As highly trained scientists, oceanographers usually enjoy good benefits, such as health insurance and retirement plans offered by their employers.

Work Environment

Oceanographers in shore stations, laboratories, and research centers work a five-day, 40-hour week. Occasionally, they serve a longer shift, particularly when a research experiment demands around-the-clock surveillance. Such assignments may also involve unusual working hours, depending on the nature of the research or the purpose of the trip. Trips at sea mean time away from home for periods extending from a few days to several months. Sea expeditions may be physically demanding and present an entirely different way of life—living on board a ship. Weather conditions may impose some hazards during these assignments. Choosing to engage in underwater research may mean a more adventuresome and hazardous way of life than in other occupations. It is wise to discover early whether or not life at sea appeals to you so that you may pursue appropriate jobs within the oceanography field.

Many jobs in oceanography, however, exist in laboratories, offices, and aquariums, with little time spent underwater or at sea. Many oceanographers are needed to analyze samples brought to land from sea; to plan, develop, and organize sea-faring trips from land; and to teach. Oceanographers who work in colleges or universities get the added benefit of the academic calendar, which provides time off for travel or research.

Outlook

Although the field of marine science is growing, researchers specializing in the popular field of biological oceanography, or marine biology, will face competition for available positions and research funding over the next few years. However, funding for graduate students and professional positions is expected to increase during the coming decade in the areas of global climate change, environmental research and management, fisheries science, and marine biomedical and pharmaceutical research programs. Although job availability is difficult to predict for several years out, anyone doing good strong academic work with a well-known professor in the field has good employment chances.

In the 1990s, the largest demand in oceanography and marine-related fields was for physical and chemical oceanographers and ocean engineers, says The Oceanographic Society. Demand and supply, however, are difficult to predict and can change according to the world market situation; for example, the state of the offshore oil market can affect demand for geological and geophysical oceanographers. You should definitely talk to your academic advisor about the current state of affairs.

The march of technology will continue to create and expand job opportunities for those interested in the marine sciences. As ways of collecting and analyzing data become more advanced, many more research positions are opening up for microbiologists, geneticists, and biochemists, fields historically restricted by the limits of technology but now rapidly expanding. All these fields can have ties to the marine biological sciences. In general, oceanographers who also have training in other sciences or in engineering will probably have better opportunities for employment than those with training limited to oceanography.

The Oceanographic Society says the growing interest in understanding and protecting the environment will also create new jobs. Careers related to fisheries resources, including basic research in biology and chemistry, as well as mariculture and sea ranching, will also increase. Because the oceans hold vast resources of commercially valuable minerals, employment opportunities will come from pharmaceutical and biotechnology companies and others interested in mining these substances for potential "miracle drugs" and other commercial uses. Continued deep-sea exploration made possible by underwater robotics and autonomous seacraft may also create more market opportunities for underwater research, with perhaps more international than U.S.-based employment potential.

Those with less education will have opportunities for employment as assistants or technicians doing more routine work. While job opportunities are currently good for marine technicians, competition is increasing and better trained or more experienced applicants have the advantage.

For More Information

For the brochure Careers in Oceanography and Marine-Related Fields, *contact:*

The Oceanography Society
4052 Timber Ridge Drive
Virginia Beach, VA 23455
Tel: 804-464-0131
Web: http://www.tos.org/tos/tos-general.html

For career information, contact these organizations:

Scripps Institution of Oceanography

0-233 University of California, San Diego
9500 Gilman Drive
La Jolla, CA 92093-0233

American Institute of Biological Sciences

1444 Eye Street, NW, Suite 200
Washington, DC 20005
Tel: 202-628-1500
Web: http://www.aibs.org/careers.html

Technical Committee on Acoustical Oceanography

Acoustical Society of America
500 Sunnyside Boulevard
Woodbury, NY 11797-2999

American Geophysical Union

2000 Florida Avenue, NW
Washington, DC 20009

Ocean Engineering Society

Institute of Electrical and Electronics Engineers
345 East 47th Street
New York, NY 10017-2394

For information about oceanography careers, contact:

About Oceanography

Texas Sea Grant College Progam
Texas A&M University
PO Box 1675
Galveston, TX 77553-1675
Web: http://www-ocean.tamu.edu/Careers/careers.html

Park Rangers

Earth science Geography	School Subjects
Helping/teaching Leadership/management	Personal Skills
Primarily outdoors Primarily multiple locations	Work Environment
Bachelor's degree	Minimum Education Level
$20,000 to $30,000 to $37,000+	Salary Range
None available	Certification or Licensing
Little change or more slowly than the average	Outlook

Overview

Park rangers enforce laws and regulations in national, state, and county parks. They help care for and maintain parks as well as inform, guide, and ensure the safety of park visitors.

History

The National Park System in the United States was begun by Congress in 1872 when Yellowstone National Park was created. The National Park Service (NPS), a bureau of the U.S. Department of the Interior, was created in 1916 to preserve, protect, and manage the national, cultural, historical, and recreational areas of the National Park System. At that time, the park system contained less than 1 million acres. Today, the country's national parks cover more than 80 million acres of mountains, plains, deserts, swamps, historic sites, lakeshores, forests, rivers, battlefields, memorials, archaeological properties, and recreation areas.

All NPS areas are given one of the following designations: National Park, National Historical Park, National Battlefield, National Battlefield Park, National Battlefield Site, National Military Site, National Memorial, National Historic Site, National Monument, National Preserve, National Seashore, National Parkway, National Lakeshore, National Reserve, National River, National Wild and Scenic River, National Recreation Area, or just Park. (The White House in Washington, DC, for example, which is administered by the NPS, is officially a Park.)

To protect the fragile, irreplaceable resources located in these areas, and to protect the millions of visitors who climb, ski, hike, boat, fish, and otherwise explore them, the National Park Service employs park rangers. State and county parks employ rangers to perform similar tasks.

The Job

Park rangers have a wide variety of duties that range from conservation efforts to bookkeeping. Their first responsibility is, however, safety. Rangers who work in parks with treacherous terrain, dangerous wildlife, or severe weather must make sure hikers, campers, and backpackers follow outdoor safety codes. They often require visitors to register at park offices so that rangers will know when someone does not return from a hike or climb and may be hurt. Rangers often participate in search-and-rescue missions for visitors who are lost or injured in parks. In mountainous or forested regions, they may use helicopters or horses for searches.

Rangers also are concerned with protecting parks from inappropriate use and other threats from humans. They register vehicles and collect parking and registration fees, which are used to help maintain roads and facilities. They enforce the laws, regulations, and policies of the parks, patrolling to prevent vandalism, theft, and harm to wildlife. Rangers may arrest and evict people who violate these laws. Some of their efforts to conserve and protect park resources include keeping jeeps and other motorized vehicles off sand dunes and other fragile lands. They make sure visitors do not litter, pollute water, chop down trees for firewood, or start unsafe campfires that could lead to catastrophic forest fires. When forest fires do start, rangers often help with the dangerous, arduous task of putting them out.

Park rangers carry out various tasks associated with the management of the natural resources within our National Park System. An important aspect of this responsibility is the care and management of both native and exotic animal species found within the boundaries of the parks. Duties may include conducting basic research, as well as disseminating information about the reintroduction of native animal populations and the protection of the natural habitat that supports the animals.

Rangers also help with conservation, research, and ecology efforts that are not connected to visitors' use of the park. They may study wildlife behavior patterns, for example, by tagging and following certain animals. In this way, they can chart the animals' migration patterns, assess the animals' impact on the park's ecosystem, and determine whether the park should take measures to control or encourage certain wildlife populations.

Some rangers study plant life and may work with conservationists to reintroduce native or endangered species. They measure the quality of water and air in the park to monitor and mitigate the effects of pollution and other threats from sources outside park boundaries.

In addition, park rangers help visitors enjoy and experience parks. In historical and other cultural parks, such as the Alamo in San Antonio, Independence Hall in Philadelphia, and the Lincoln Home in Springfield, Illinois, rangers give lectures and provide guided tours explaining the history and significance of the site. In natural parks, they may lecture on conservation topics, provide information about plants and animals in the park, and take visitors on interpretive walks, pointing out the area's flora, fauna, and geological characteristics. At a Civil War battlefield park, such as Gettysburg National Military Park in Pennsylvania or Vicksburg National Military Park in Mississippi, they explain to visitors what happened at that site during the Civil War and its implications for our country.

Park rangers are also indispensable to the management and administration of parks. They issue permits to visitors and vehicles and help plan the recreational activities in parks. They are involved with planning and managing park budgets. They keep records and compile statistics concerning weather conditions, resource conservation activities, and the number of park visitors.

Many rangers supervise other workers in the parks—those who build and maintain park facilities, work part time or seasonally, or operate concession facilities. Rangers often have their own park maintenance responsibilities, such as trail building, landscaping, and caring for visitor centers.

In some parks, rangers are specialists in certain areas of park protection, safety, or management. For example, in areas with heavy snowfalls and a high incidence of avalanches, experts in avalanche control and snow safety are designated *snow rangers*. They monitor snow conditions and patrol park areas to make sure visitors are not lost in snowslides.

Requirements

High School

High school students preparing for the necessary college courses should take earth science, mathematics, English, and speech. Any classes or activities that deal with plant and animal life, the weather, geography, and interacting with others will be helpful.

Postsecondary Training

Employment as a federal or state park ranger requires either a college degree or a specific amount of education and experience. Approximately 200 colleges and universities offer bachelor's degree programs in park management and park recreation. To meet employment requirements, students in other relevant college programs must accumulate at least 24 semester hours of academic credit in park recreation and management, history, behavioral science, forestry, botany, geology, or other applicable subject areas.

Without a degree, applicants need three years of experience in parks or conservation and must show they understand what is required in park work. In addition, they must demonstrate good communication skills. A combination of education and experience can also fulfill job requirements, with one academic year of study equalling nine months of experience. Also, the orientation and training a ranger receives on the job may be supplemented with formal training courses.

Rangers need skills in protecting forests, parks, and wildlife and in interpreting natural or historical resources. Law enforcement and management skills are also important. Rangers who wish to move into management positions may need graduate degrees. Approximately 50 universities offer master's degrees in park recreation and management and 16 have doctoral programs.

Other Requirements

The right kind of person to fill a park ranger position believes in the importance of the country's park resources and the mission of the park system. People who enjoy working outdoors—independently and with others—may enjoy park ranger work. Rangers need self-confidence, patience, and the ability to stay levelheaded during emergencies. Those who participate in rescues need courage, physical stamina, and endurance, while those who deal with visitors need tact, sincerity, personable natures, and a sense of humor. A sense of camaraderie among fellow rangers also can add to the enjoyment of being a park ranger.

Exploring

Persons interested in exploring park ranger work may wish to apply for part-time or seasonal work in national, state, or county parks. Such workers usually perform maintenance and other unskilled tasks, but they have opportunities to observe park rangers and talk with them about their work. Interested persons also may wish to work as volunteers. Many park research activities, study projects, and rehabilitation efforts are conducted by volunteer groups affiliated with universities or conservation organizations, and these activities can provide insight into the work done by park rangers.

Employers

Park rangers in the National Park Service are employed by the U.S. Department of the Interior. Other rangers may be employed by other federal agencies or by state and county agencies in charge of their respective parks.

Starting Out

Many workers enter national park ranger jobs after working part time or seasonally at different parks. These workers often work at information desks or in fire control or law enforcement positions. Some help maintain trails, collect trash, or perform forestry activities. Persons interested in applying for park ranger jobs with the federal government should contact their local Federal Job Information Center or the Federal Office of Personnel Management in Washington, DC, for application information. Those people seeking jobs in state parks should write to the appropriate state departments for information.

Advancement

Nearly all rangers start in entry-level positions, which means that nearly all higher-level openings are filled by the promotion of current workers. Entry-level rangers may move into positions as district rangers or park managers, or they may become specialists in resource management or park planning. Rangers who show management skills and become park managers may have opportunities to move into administrative positions in the district, regional, or national headquarters.

The orientation and training a ranger receives on the job may be supplemented with formal training courses. Training for job skills unique to the National Park Service is available at the Horace M. Albright Training Center at Grand Canyon National Park in Arizona and the Stephen T. Mather Training Center at Harpers Ferry, West Virginia. In addition, the NPS makes use of training facilities at the Federal Law Enforcement Training Center in Brunswick, Georgia.

Earnings

Rangers in the National Park Service are usually hired at the GS-5 grade level, with a salary of around $20,000. More experienced or educated rangers may enter the Park Service at the GS-9 level, which pays approximately $30,000 to start. The government may provide housing to rangers who work in remote areas.

Rangers in state parks work for the state government. They receive comparable salaries and benefits, including paid vacations, sick leave, paid holidays, health and life insurance, and pension plans.

Work Environment

Rangers work in parks all over the country, from the Okefenokee Swamp in Florida to the Rocky Mountains of Colorado. They work in the mountains and forests of Hawaii, Alaska, and California and in urban and suburban parks throughout the United States.

National park rangers are hired to work 40 hours per week, but their actual working hours can be long and irregular, with a great deal of overtime. They may receive extra pay or time off for working overtime. Some rangers are on call 24 hours a day for emergencies. During the peak tourist seasons, rangers work longer hours. Although many rangers work in offices, many also work outside in all kinds of climates and weather, and most work in a combination of the two settings. Workers may be called upon to risk their own health to rescue injured visitors in cold, snow, rain, and darkness. Rangers in Alaska must adapt to long daylight hours in the summer and short daylight hours in the winter. Working outdoors in beautiful surroundings, however, can be wonderfully stimulating and rewarding for the right kind of worker.

Outlook

Park ranger jobs are scarce, and competition for them is fierce. The U.S. Park Service has reported that the ratio of applicants to available positions is sometimes as high as one hundred to one. As a result, applicants should attain the greatest number and widest variety of applicable skills possible. They may wish to study subjects they can use in other fields: forestry, land management, conservation, wildlife management, history, and natural sciences, for example.

The scarcity of openings is expected to continue indefinitely. Job seekers, therefore, may wish to apply for outdoor work with agencies other than the National Park Service, including other federal land and resource management agencies and similar state and local agencies. Such agencies usually have more openings.

For More Information

National Association of State Park Directors
9894 East Holden Place
Tucson, AZ 85748
Tel: 520-298-4924

National Recreation and Park Association
22377 Belmont Ridge Road
Ashburn, VA 20148-4510
Tel: 703-858-0784
Web: http://www.nrpa.org

National Parks and Conservation Association
1776 Massachusetts Avenue, NW
Washington, DC 20036
Tel: 202-223-6722
Web: http://www.npca.org/npca

Student Conservation Association
PO Box 550
Charlestown, NH 03603-0550
Tel: 603-543-1700
Web: http://www.sca-inc.org

Pollution Control Technicians

Biology Chemistry	School Subjects
Mechanical/manipulative Technical/scientific	Personal Skills
Indoors and outdoors One location with some travel	Work Environment
Some postsecondary training	Minimum Education Level
$15,500 to $28,500 to $49,500+	Salary Range
Required for certain positions	Certification or Licensing
About as fast as the average	Outlook

Overview

Pollution control technicians, also known as *environmental technicians,* conduct tests and field investigations to obtain samples and data required by engineers, scientists, and others to clean up, monitor, control, or prevent pollution. They apply principles and methods of engineering, chemistry, meteorology, agriculture, or other disciplines in their work. A pollution control technician usually specializes in air, water, or soil pollution. Although work differs by employer and specialty, technicians generally collect samples for laboratory analysis, using specialized instruments and equipment; monitor pollution control devices and systems, such as smokestack air "scrubbers"; and perform various other tests and investigations to evaluate pollution problems. They follow strict procedures in collecting and recording data in order to meet the requirements of environmental laws.

In general, pollution control technicians do not operate the equipment and systems designed to prevent pollution or remove pollutants. Instead, they test environmental conditions. In addition, some analyze and report on their findings.

History

Stricter pollution control regulations of the mid-1960s to early 1970s created a job market for pollution control technicians. As regulations on industry have become more stringent, the job of pollution control technician has grown both in numbers and in scope. For centuries, the biosphere (the self-regulating "envelope" of air, water, and land in which all life on earth exists) was generally able to scatter, break down, or adapt all the wastes and pollution produced by people.

This began to change drastically with the Industrial Revolution. Begun in England in the 1750s, the Industrial Revolution was the shift from a farming society to an industrialized society. Although it had many economic benefits, it took a terrible toll on the environment. Textile manufacturing and then iron processing spread through England, and coal-powered mills, machines, and factories spewed heavy black smoke into the air. Rivers and lakes became open sewers as factories dumped their wastes anywhere. By the 19th century, areas with high population density and clusters of factories were experiencing markedly higher death and disease rates than areas with little industrial development.

The Industrial Revolution spread all over the world, including France in the 1830s; Germany in the 1850s; the United States after the Civil War; Asia (especially Japan), beginning at the turn of the century; and Russia, beginning after the Russian Revolution of 1917. Wherever industry took hold, there were warning signs that the biosphere could not handle the resulting pollution. Smog hung over large cities with many factories. Residents experienced more respiratory and other health problems. Manufacturing wastes and untreated sewage poisoned surface waters and underground sources of water, affecting drinking-water supplies and increasing disease. Wastes and pollution also seeped into the soil, affecting crops.

After World War II, the development of new synthetic materials including plastics, pesticides, and other substances that were more toxic or more difficult to degrade (break down) worsened pollution problems. So did vehicle exhaust. Fish and wildlife were dying; rivers and lakes were choked with chemicals and wastes. Scientists documented connections between pollution and birth defects, cancer, fertility problems, genetic damage, and many other serious problems.

Not until the mid-1960s to early 1970s did public outcry, environmental activism, and political and economic necessity force the passage of stricter pollution control laws. Federal environmental legislation mandated cleanups of existing air, water, and soil pollution and began to limit the type and amount of polluting substances that industry could release to the environment. Manufacturers began to be required to operate within strict guidelines for air emissions, process-wastewater treatment and disposal, and other polluting activities. States and municipalities also were given increasing responsibilities for monitoring and working to reduce levels of auto, industrial, and other pollution. Out of the need to meet these new requirements, the U.S. pollution control industry was born-and with it, the job of pollution control technician.

The Job

Technicians usually specialize in one aspect of pollution control and are categorized as water pollution control technicians, air pollution control technicians, or soil pollution control technicians. Sampling, monitoring, and testing are the major activities of the job. No matter what the specialty, pollution control technicians work largely for or with government agencies that regulate pollution by industry.

Increasingly, pollution control technicians input their data into computers. Instruments used to collect water samples or monitor water sources may be highly sophisticated electronic devices. Technicians usually do not analyze the data they collect. However, they may report on what they know to scientists or engineers, either verbally or in writing.

Water pollution control technicians monitor both industrial and residential discharge, such as from wastewater treatment plants. Soil pollution technicians may work in rural areas, where the concern is how substances in the soil enter into crops for human consumption. Water pollution control technicians help to determine the presence and extent of pollutants in water. They collect water samples from lakes, streams, rivers, or other surface waters; groundwater (the water under the earth); industrial or municipal wastewater; or other sources. Samples are brought to labs, where chemical and other tests are performed to analyze them. If the samples contain harmful substances, remedial (cleanup) actions will need to be taken. Technicians also may perform various field tests, such as checking the pH, oxygen, and nitrate level of surface waters.

Some water pollution control technicians set up monitoring equipment to obtain information on water flow, movement, temperature, pressure, or other factors and record readings from these devices. To trace flow patterns, they may introduce dyes into the water.

Water pollution control technicians have to be careful not to contaminate their samples, stray from the specific testing procedure, or otherwise do something to ruin the sample or cause faulty or misleading results.

Depending on the specific job, water pollution control technicians may spend a good part of their time outdoors, in good weather and bad, aboard boats, and sometimes near unpleasant smells or potentially hazardous substances. Field sites may be scattered or remote places; in some cases it may be necessary to fly to a different part of the country (especially if the technician works for a private consulting firm), perhaps staying away from home for a long period of time. Water pollution control technicians play a big role in industrial wastewater discharge monitoring, treatment, and control. Nearly every manufacturing process produces wastewater, but U.S. manufacturers today must be more careful about what they discharge with their wastewater.

Some water technicians specialize in groundwater, ocean water, or other types of natural waters. *Estuarine resource technicians,* for example, specialize in estuary waters, or coastal areas where fresh water and salt water come together. These bays, salt marshes, inlets, and other tidal water bodies support a wide variety of plant and animal life with ecologically complex relationships. They are vulnerable to destructive pollution from adjoining industries, cities and towns, and other sources. Estuarine resource technicians aid scientists in studying the resulting environmental changes. They may work in laboratories or aboard boats, or clad in diving gear in the water. They operate, maintain, and calibrate instruments; collect and analyze water samples; record observations; and perform other tasks that are part of investigating estuarine habitats and their organisms.

Air pollution control technicians collect and test air samples, such as from stacks or chimneys of industrial manufacturing plants; record data on atmospheric conditions, such as to help a city determine levels of airborne substances from auto or industrial emissions; and supply data to scientists and engineers for further testing and analysis. In labs, air pollution control technicians may help test air samples or re-create contaminants. They may use atomic absorption spectrophotometers, flame photometers, gas chromatographs, and other instruments for analyzing samples.

In the field, air pollution control technicians may utilize rooftop sampling devices or operate mobile monitoring units or stationary trailers. The trailers may be equipped with elaborate, continuously operating automatic testing systems, including some of the same devices found in laboratories. Outside air is pumped into various chambers in the trailer where it is analyzed for the presence of pollutants. The results may be recorded by machine on 30-day rolls of graph paper or fed into a computer at regular intervals. Technicians may set up and maintain the sampling devices, replenish the chemicals used in tests, replace worn parts, calibrate instruments, and record results. Some air pollution control technicians specialize in certain pollutants or pollution sources. For example, *engine emission technicians* focus on exhaust from internal combustion engines.

Soil pollution control technicians collect soil, silt, or mud samples so they can be checked for contamination. Soil can become contaminated when polluted water seeps into the earth, such as when liquid waste (leachate) leaks from a landfill or other source into surrounding ground. Soil pollution control technicians work for federal, state, and local government agencies, for private consulting firms, and elsewhere. (Some *soil conservation technicians* perform pollution control work.)

A position sometimes grouped with other pollution control technicians is that of noise pollution control technician. *Noise pollution control technicians* use rooftop devices and mobile units to take readings and collect data on noise levels of factories, highways, airports, and other locations in order to determine noise exposure levels for workers or the public. Some test noise levels of construction equipment, chain saws, snow blowers, lawn mowers, or other equipment.

Requirements

High School

In high school, key courses include biology, chemistry, and physics. Conservation or ecology courses also will be useful. Math classes should include at least algebra and geometry. English, speech, communications, or other language arts classes will help sharpen written and oral communication skills, necessary in any job. Computer classes are also helpful.

Postsecondary Training

Some technician positions call for a high school degree plus employer training. As pollution control becomes more technical and complex, more positions are awarded to technicians with at least an associate's degree. To meet this need, many community colleges across the country have developed appropriate programs for pollution control technicians. Areas of study include environmental engineering technologies, pollution control technologies, air pollution control technologies, conservation, ecology, and others. A future air pollution control technician, for example, might take courses in meteorology, toxicology, source testing, sampling and analysis, air quality management, technical math, chemistry, communications skills, physics, air pollution instrumentation, sources of air pollution, air pollution control, biology, environmental science, computers, and statistics. The exact degree or other training required varies by employer. Some experts advise attending school in the part of the country where you'd like to begin your career so you can start getting to know local employers before you graduate.

Certification or Licensing

Certification or licensing is required for some positions in pollution control, especially those in which sanitation, public health, a public water supply, or a sewage treatment system is involved.

Other Requirements

Pollution control technicians should be patient, detail oriented, capable of following instructions, and curious. Basic manual skills are a must for collecting samples and performing similar tasks. Today, often-complex environmental regulations drive technicians' jobs; therefore, it's crucial to be able to read and understand technical materials and to follow to the letter any written guidelines for sampling or other procedures. Computer skills, as well as skills in reading and interpreting maps, charts, and diagrams, are also a help.

Technicians must make accurate and objective observations, maintain clear and complete records of data, and do certain types of computations. Good physical conditioning is a requirement for some activities, such as climbing up smokestacks to take emission samples.

Exploring

Students who want to learn about jobs in pollution control can begin by visiting a large library and reading technical and general-interest publications in environmental science. This will give you an idea of the technologies being used and issues being discussed. You also can visit a municipal health department or pollution control agency in your community. Many agencies are pleased to explain their work to visitors.

School science clubs, local community groups, and naturalist clubs may help broaden your understanding of various aspects of the natural world and allow you to take an in-depth look at a few specific areas of interest. Most schools have recycling programs that enlist student help.

A tour of a local manufacturing plant using an air- or water-pollution abatement system also might be arranged. Many plants offer tours of their operations to the public. Taking such a tour would provide an excellent opportunity to see the equipment and conditions technicians work with.

As a high school student, it may be difficult to obtain summer or part-time work as a technician, due to the extensive operations and safety training required for some of these jobs. However, it is worthwhile to check with a local environmental agency, nonprofit environmental organizations, or private consulting firms to learn of volunteer or paid support opportunities. Any hands-on experience you can get will be of value to a future employer.

Employers

Many jobs for pollution control technicians are with the government agencies that monitor the environment, such as the Environmental Protection Agency and the Departments of Agriculture, Energy, and Interior.

Water pollution control technicians may be employed by manufacturers that produce wastewater; municipal wastewater treatment facilities; consultants or other private firms hired to monitor or control pollutants in water or wastewater; pollution control equipment and supply manufacturers that make filters, chemicals, or other products to eliminate or reduce the level of harmful substances in water or wastewater; or government regulatory agencies responsible for protecting water quality, including monitoring local water and wastewater.

Air pollution control technicians work for government agencies, including regional EPA offices, as well as private manufacturers producing airborne pollutants; consultants; research facilities; air pollution control equipment manufacturers; and other employers.

Soil pollution control technicians may work for federal or state departments of agriculture, federal or regional EPA offices, or for private agricultural groups that monitor soil quality for pesticide levels.

Noise pollution control technicians are employed by private companies and by government agencies such as OSHA (Occupational Safety and Health Administration).

Starting Out

Graduates of two-year pollution control technology or related programs are often employed during their final term by recruiters who visit their schools. Specific opportunities will vary depending on the part of the country, the segment of the environmental industry, the specialization of the technician (air, water, land), the economy, and other factors. When they first start out, technicians may find the greatest number of positions available in state or local government agencies. One career path is to start out working for a state or local government agenc, and then move on to higher-paying jobs in the private sector.

Most schools can provide job-hunting advice and assistance. Direct application to state or local environmental agencies, employment agencies, or potential employers can also be a productive approach. Students hoping to find employment outside their current geographic areas may get good results by checking with professional organizations or by reading advertisements in technical journals, many of which have searchable job listings on the Internet.

Advancement

The typical hierarchy for pollution control work is technician (two years of postsecondary education or less), technologist (two years or more of postsecondary training), technician manager (perhaps a technician or technologist with many years of experience), and scientist or engineer (four-year bachelor of science degree or more, up to Ph.D. level).

In some private manufacturing or consulting firms, technician positions are used for training newly recruited professional staff. In such cases, workers with four-year degrees in engineering or physical science are likely to be promoted before those with two-year degrees. Employees of government agencies usually are organized under civil service systems that specify experience, education, and other criteria for advancement. Private industry promotions are structured differently and will depend on a variety of factors.

Earnings

Pay for pollution control technicians varies widely depending on the nature of the work they do, training and experience required for the work, type of employer, geographic region, demand for technicians compared to available supply, and other factors. Public-sector positions tend to pay less than private-sector positions.

Government entry-level salaries for pollution control technicians are about $15,500 to $19,500 per year, depending on education and experience. The average is $28,500 per year. Technicians who move up to become managers or supervisors can make up to $49,500 per year or more. Technicians who further their education to secure teaching positions can also expect to earn higher than the average wage.

No matter which area they specialize in, pollution control technicians generally enjoy fringe benefits such as paid vacation, holidays and sick time, and employer-paid training. Technicians who work full time (and some who work part time) often have employer-paid health insurance benefits. Technicians who are employed by the federal government may get additional benefits, which may or may not be paid by private employers, such as pension and retirement benefits.

Work Environment

Conditions range from clean and pleasant indoor offices and laboratories to outdoor, hot or cold, wet, bad-smelling, noisy, even hazardous situations. Anyone planning a career in pollution control technology should realize the possibility of exposure to unpleasant conditions at least occasionally in his or her career. Employers often can minimize these negatives through special equipment and procedures. Most laboratories and manufacturing companies have safety procedures for potentially dangerous situations.

Some jobs involve vigorous physical activity (for example, handling a small boat or climbing ladders on smokestacks). For the most part, technicians need only be able to do moderate activity. Travel may be required. It may be necessary to go to urban, industrial, or rural settings for sampling.

Because technicians' jobs can involve a considerable amount of repetitive work, patience and the ability to handle routine are important. Yet, particularly when they are working in the field, pollution control technicians also have to be ready to use their resourcefulness and ingenuity to find the best ways of responding to new situations.

Technicians need to be able to communicate with others—including fellow technicians, supervisors, scientists, and engineers, and in some positions, clients, the public, regulatory officials, and others . They should work well alone or as part of a team.

Outlook

Demand for technicians is expected to increase about as fast as the average through 2006. Those trained to handle increasingly complex technical demands will have the upper hand. All science technicians (including medical science, agricultural, pollution control) held about 228,000 jobs in 1996. While other technicians were employed by manufacturing (largely the chemical industry), the federal government employed 16,000 science technicians, largely pollution control technicians, in 1996. The government predicts that 258,000 science technicians will be employed in 2006, a 12.9 percent increase for all science technicians.

Demand will be higher in some areas of the country than others depending on specialty; for example, air pollution control technicians will be especially in demand in large cities facing pressure to comply with national air quality standards (Los Angeles, New York). Amount of industrialization, stringency of state and local pollution control enforcement, local economy, and other factors also will affect demand by region and specialty. Perhaps the single greatest factor affecting all pollution control work is the federal government's continued mandate for pollution control. As long as the federal government is supporting pollution control, the pollution control industry will continue to grow and technicians will be needed.

For More Information

The following organizations' members work in air pollution control, hazardous waste management, and groundwater quality control:

Air and Waste Management Association
One Gateway Center, Third Floor
Pittsburgh, PA 15222
Tel: 412-232-3444
Web: http://www.awma.org

National Ground Water Association
601 Dempsey Road
Westerville, OH 43081
Tel: 614-898-7791
Web: http://www.ngwa.org

Following is the national organization. For your state's Environmental Protection Agency, check the government listings in your phone book:

Environmental Protection Agency
401 M Street, SW
Washington, DC 20460
Tel: 202-260-2090
Web: http://www.epa.gov

The following organization is an environmental careers resource for high school and college students:

Environmental Careers Organization
179 South Street
Boston, MA 02111
Tel: 617-426-4375
Web: http://www.eco.org

Water Environment Federation
601 Wythe Street
Alexandria, VA 22314-1994
Tel: 703-684-2452
Web: http://www.wef.org

Range Managers

School Subjects	Biology Earth science
Personal Skills	Leadership/management Technical/scientific
Work Environment	Indoors and outdoors Primarily multiple locations
Minimum Education Level	Bachelor's degree
Salary Range	$17,200 to $25,000 to $34,000
Certification or Licensing	None available
Outlook	About as fast as the average

Overview

Range managers work to maintain and improve grazing lands on public and private property. They research, develop, and carry out methods to improve and increase the production of forage plants, livestock, and wildlife without damaging the environment; develop and carry out plans for water facilities, erosion control, and soil treatments; restore rangelands that have been damaged by fire, pests, and undesirable plants; and manage the upkeep of range improvements, such as fences, corrals, and reservoirs.

History

Early in the history of the world, primitive peoples grazed their livestock wherever forage was plentiful. As the supply of grass and shrubs became depleted, they simply moved on, leaving the stripped land to suffer the effects of soil erosion. When civilization grew and the nomadic tribes began to establish settlements, people began to recognize the need for conservation, and they developed simple methods of land terracing, irrigation, and rotation of grazing lands.

Much the same thing happened in the United States. The rapid expansion across the continent in the 19th century was accompanied by the destruction of plant and animal life and the abuse of the soil. Because the country's natural resources appeared inexhaustible, the cries of alarm that came from a few concerned conservationists went unheeded. It was not until after 1890 that conservation became a national policy. Today several state and federal agencies are actively involved in protecting the nation's soil, water, forests, and wildlife.

Rangelands cover more than a billion acres of the United States, mostly in the western states and Alaska. Many natural resources are found there: grass and shrubs for animal grazing, wildlife habitats, water from vast watersheds, recreation facilities, and valuable mineral and energy resources. In addition, rangelands are used by scientists who study the environment.

The Job

Range managers are sometimes known as *range scientists, range ecologists,* or *range conservationists.* Their goal is to maximize range resources without damaging the environment. They accomplish this in a number of ways.

To help ranchers attain optimum livestock production, range managers study the rangelands to determine the number and kind of livestock that can be most profitably grazed, the grazing system to use, and the best seasons for grazing. The systems they recommend must be designed to conserve the soil and vegetation for other uses, such as wildlife habitats, outdoor recreation, and timber.

Grazing lands must continually be restored and improved. Range managers study plants to determine which varieties are best suited to a particular range and to develop improved methods for reseeding. They devise biological, chemical, or mechanical ways of controlling undesirable and poisonous plants, and they design methods of protecting the range from grazing damage.

Range managers also develop and help carry out plans for water facilities, structures for erosion control, and soil treatments. They are responsible for the construction and maintenance of such improvements as fencing, corrals, and reservoirs for stock watering.

Although a great deal of range managers' time is spent outdoors, they also spend some time in offices, consulting with other conservation specialists, preparing written reports, and doing administrative work.

Rangelands have more than one use, so range managers often work in such closely related fields as wildlife and watershed management, forest management, and recreation. *Soil conservationists* and *naturalists* are concerned with maintaining ecological balance both on the range and in the forest preserves.

Requirements

High School

High school students who are interested in pursuing a career in range management should begin planning their education early. Courses in science, mathematics, English, economics, and computer science are good preparation for college studies.

Postsecondary Training

The minimum educational requirement for range managers is usually a bachelor's degree in range management or range science. To be hired by the federal government, graduates need at least 42 credit hours in plant, animal, or soil sciences and natural resources management courses, including at least 18 hours in range management. For teaching and research positions, graduate degrees in range management are generally mandatory. Advanced degrees may also prove helpful for advancement in other jobs.

To receive a degree in range management, students must have acquired a basic knowledge of biology, chemistry, physics, mathematics, and communication skills. Specialized courses in range management combine plant, animal, and soil sciences with the principles of ecology and resource management. Students in degree programs are also encouraged to take electives, such as economics, forestry, hydrology, agronomy, wildlife, and computer science.

While a number of schools offer some courses related to range management, only about 18 colleges and universities have degree programs in range management or range science.

Other Requirements

Along with their technical skills, range managers must be able to speak and write effectively and to work well with others. Range managers need to be self-motivated and flexible. They are generally persons who do not want the restrictions of an office setting and a rigid schedule. They should have a love for the outdoors as well as good health and physical stamina for the strenuous activity that this occupation requires.

Exploring

High school students considering a career in range management may test their appetite for outdoor work by applying for summer jobs on ranches or farms. Other ways of exploring this occupation include a field trip to a ranch or interviews with or lectures by range managers, ranchers, or conservationists. Any volunteer work with conservation organizations—large or small— will give you an idea of what range managers do and will help you when you apply to colleges and for employment.

College students can get more direct experience by applying for summer jobs in range management with such federal agencies as the Forest Service, the Soil Conservation Service, and the Bureau of Land Management. This experience may better qualify them for jobs when they graduate.

Employers

Between 8,000 and 10,000 range managers are currently employed. The federal government employs most of them in the agencies mentioned above, while state governments employ range managers in game and fish departments, state land agencies, and extension services.

In private industry, the number of range managers is increasing. They work for coal and oil companies to help reclaim mined areas, for banks and real estate firms to help increase the revenue from landholdings, and for private consulting firms and large ranches. Some range managers with advanced degrees teach and do research at colleges and universities. Others work overseas with U.S. and U.N. agencies and with foreign governments.

Starting Out

The usual way to enter this occupation is to apply directly to the appropriate government agencies. People interested in working for the federal government may contact the Department of Agriculture's Forest Service or Soil Conservation Service, or the Department of the Interior's Bureau of Indian Affairs or Bureau of Land Management. Others may apply to local state employment offices for jobs in state land agencies, game and fish departments, or agricultural extension services. College placement offices have listings of available jobs.

Advancement

Range managers may advance to administrative positions in which they plan and supervise the work of others and write reports. Others may go into teaching or research. It should be remembered that an advanced degree is often necessary for the higher-level jobs in this occupational field. Another way for range managers to advance is to enter business for themselves as *range management consultants* or *ranchers*.

Earnings

Experienced range managers with the federal government earn an average of about $34,000 a year. Those with bachelor's degrees can expect starting salaries in the range of $17,200 to $21,300 a year. State governments and private companies pay their range managers salaries that are about the same as those paid by the federal government. Range managers are also eligible for paid vacations and sick days, health and life insurance, and other benefits.

Work Environment

Range managers, particularly those just beginning their careers, spend a great deal of time on the range. That means they must work outdoors in all kinds of weather. They usually travel by car or small plane, but in rough country they use four-wheel-drive vehicles or get around on horseback or on foot. When riding the range, managers may spend a considerable amount of time away from home, and the work is often quite strenuous.

As range managers advance to administrative jobs, they spend more time working in offices, writing reports, and planning and supervising the work of others. Range managers may work alone or under direct supervision; often they work as part of a team. In any case, they must deal constantly with people—not only their superiors and co-workers but with the general public, ranchers, government officials, and other conservation specialists.

Outlook

This is a small occupation, and most of the openings will arise when older, experienced range managers retire or leave the field. Job growth will be about the same as the average for all occupations in the next decade. The need for range managers should be stimulated by a growing demand for wildlife habitats, recreation, and water as well as by an increasing concern for the environment. A greater number of large ranches will employ range managers to improve range management practices and increase output and profitability. Range specialists will also be employed in larger numbers by private industry to reclaim lands damaged by oil and coal exploration.

An additional demand for range managers could be created by the conversion of rangelands to other purposes, such as wildlife habitats and recreation. Federal employment for these activities, however, depends upon the passage of legislation concerning the management of range resources, an area that is always controversial. Smaller budgets may also limit employment growth in this area.

For More Information

Career information and a list of schools offering range management training may be obtained from:

National Recreation and Park Association
22377 Belmont Ridge Road
Ashburn, VA 20148-4510
Tel: 703-858-0784
Web: http://www.nrpa.org/nrpa

To obtain career and educational information concerning range management, contact:

Society for Range Management
1839 York Street
Denver, CO 80206
Tel: 303-355-7070

For information about career opportunities in the federal government, write to:

U.S. Department of Agriculture
U.S. Forest Service
14th Street and Independence Avenue, SW
Washington, DC 20250
Tel: 202-205-8333

U.S. Department of Agriculture
Soil Conservation Service
PO Box 2890
Washington, DC 20013
Tel: 202-205-0026

U.S. Department of the Interior
Bureau of Land Management
1849 C Street, NW
Washington, DC 20240
Tel: 202-452-5120

Recycling Coordinators

	School Subjects
Business Earth science	
	Personal Skills
Communication/ideas Leadership/management	
	Work Environment
Primarily indoors Multiple locations	
	Minimum Education Level
Bachelor's degree	
	Salary Range
$22,000 to $40,000 to $50,000+	
	Certification or Licensing
None available	
	Outlook
Much faster than the average	

Overview

Recycling coordinators manage recycling programs for city, county, or state governments or large organizations, such as colleges or military bases. They work with waste haulers and material recovery facilities (MRFs) to arrange for collecting, sorting, and processing recyclables—such as aluminum, glass, and paper—from households and businesses. Recycling coordinators are also often responsible for educating the public about the value of recycling as well as instructing residents on how to properly separate recyclables in their homes. Recycling coordinators keep records of recycling rates in their municipality and help set goals for diversion of recyclables from the waste stream.

History

Recycling coordinators have a brief history in the job as it is known today. Only in the 1980s and early 1990s did many states begin setting recycling goals, creating the need for recycling coordinators at the local level. Prior to that time, there was little need for municipal recycling coordinators. Most recycling efforts were made by private citizen groups or industry. While much of today's recycling is driven by a desire to improve the environment, earlier recycling was often driven by economic forces. During the Great Depression, individual citizens or groups, such as the Boy Scouts, held newspaper drives and turned the newspaper in to a recycler. The recycler paid a minimal amount for the collection of the newspapers and then generally sold the newspaper to industry, which recycled or otherwise reused the newspaper. During World War II, shortages in raw materials to support the war effort prompted citizens to hold drives for aluminum, rubber, paper and scrap metal; this time the spirit of recycling was patriotic, as well as economic.

Other than in times of shortage, governments had little concern with how people disposed of waste, simply because there was relatively little waste. Municipalities had been dumping, burning, burying, or otherwise disposing of residents' waste for years with little consequence. In 1898, New York City opened the first garbage-sorting plant in the United States, recycling some of the trash. The first aluminum recycling plants were built in the early 1900s in Chicago and Cleveland. By the 1920s, about 70 percent of U.S. cities had limited recycling programs, according to the League of Women Voters.

Can buybacks began in the 1950s; newspaper was first recycled in 1961 by a mill in New Jersey. By 1960, the U.S. recycled about 7 percent of its municipal waste. In the mid-1960s, the federal government began to take greater interest in municipal waste-handling methods. Part of the Solid Waste Disposal Act of 1965 granted money for states to develop waste-handling programs. The Resource Conservation and Recovery Act (RCRA) of 1970 and 1976 amendments defined types of municipal solid waste (MSW) and spelled out minimum standards for waste handling.

State and federal governments, such as branches of the Environmental Protection Agency, were the earliest to hire people who specialized in recycling. These recycling experts usually acted in an advisory capacity to local governments that were trying to develop their own programs.

In the 1990s, more states began to set recycling goals, driving the increase in need for recycling coordinators. By 1998, all but six states had set formal recycling goals. These goals are generally stated in terms of the percentage of waste to be diverted from ending up in a landfill. Most states set goals between 20 and 50 percent. To encourage counties to make the effort at a local level, many state governments offered grants to counties to fund new recycling programs, hence many counties found they needed a full-time person to coordinate the new effort. Initially, only the most populous counties qualified for the grants to afford a recycling program because they could divert the highest volume from landfills.

The Job

As recycling becomes more widespread, fewer recycling coordinators are faced with the task of organizing a municipal program from scratch. Instead, recycling coordinators work to improve current recycling rates in several ways. While recycling coordinators spend some time on administrative tasks, such as meeting with waste haulers and government officials and writing reports, a considerable amount of time is often needed for public education purposes. One recycling coordinator in North Dakota notes that only a small portion of the average recycling coordinator's job is spent sitting behind a desk.

Educating the public on proper separation of recyclables as well as explaining the need for recycling are a large part of a recycling coordinator's job. Good oral communication skills are essential for a recycling coordinator to succeed in this role. Getting people who haven't recycled before to start can take some convincing. Recycling coordinators spread their message by speaking to community groups, businesses, and schools. Persuasive speaking skills are useful here, because as a recycling coordinator, you are asking people to do extra work—peeling labels from and washing bottles and jars instead of just throwing them out, separating newspapers, magazines, cardboard, and other types of paper. Even as recycling increases in this country, many people are accustomed to disposing of trash as quickly as possible without giving it a second thought. It is the task of a recycling coordinator to get people to change such habits, and how well a recycling coordinator is able to do this can make the difference in the success of the entire program.

In some communities, recycling coordinators have economics on their side when it comes to getting people to change their habits. In so-called "pay-as-you-throw" programs, residents pay for garbage disposal based on how much waste their household produces. So recycling, although it may mean extra work, makes sense because it saves the homeowner money. For example, residents may be charged extra for any waste they set out at the curb beyond one garbage can per week. In communities with these programs, recycling rates tend to be higher and recycling coordinators have an easier task of convincing people to recycle. Another part of a recycling coordinator's role as educator is answering questions about how recyclables are to be separated. Especially with new programs, residents often have questions about separating recyclables, such as what type of paper can be set out with newspaper, whether labels should be peeled from jars, and even keeping track of which week of the month or day of the week they should set their recyclables out with the trash. Fielding these types of calls always demands some portion of a recycling coordinator's time.

Most recycling coordinators spend a minimal amount of time on record keeping, perhaps 5 percent, one coordinator estimates. The coordinator is responsible for making monthly, or sometimes quarterly, reports to state and federal government agencies. Recycling coordinators also fill out grant applications for state and federal funding to improve their programs.

Some recycling coordinators work on military bases or college campuses. The goal of a recycling coordinator who works in one of these settings is the same as a municipal recycling coordinator—getting people to recycle; how they go about it may differ. The recycling coordinator on a college campus, for example, has a new set of residents every year to educate about the college's recycling program.

Recycling coordinators who come up with creative uses for waste may find opportunities in other fields as well. For example, recycling of computers and computer parts is a growing area. Some with knowledge in this area have founded their own companies or work for computer manufacturers.

Requirements

High School

Recycling coordinators need a variety of skills and doing well in a variety of classes in high school is a good start. Classes in business, economics, and civics are a good idea to help build an understanding of the public sector in which most recycling coordinators work. Knowledge of how local governments and markets for recycled materials function are things a recycling coordinator will need to know later, and civics and economics courses provide this framework. English and speech classes are vital to developing good oral and written communication skills that recycling coordinators use to spread the word about the importance of recycling. Mathematics and science will prove useful in setting recycling goals and understanding how recycling helps the environment.

Postsecondary Training

Until recently, people with all different types of backgrounds and experience were becoming recycling coordinators. Enthusiasm, an understanding of recycling issues, and business acumen were more important than any specific degree or professional background. This is still true to some extent, as colleges generally don't offer degrees in recycling coordination. Instead, a bachelor's degree in environmental studies or a related area and strong communication skills are desirable. Some schools offer minors in integrated waste management. Classes may include public policy, source reduction, transformation technology (composting/waste energy), and landfills, according to the Environmental Careers Organization (ECO).

Other Requirements

Useful personal skills include good communication and people skills for interacting with staff, contractors, government officials, and the public. Leadership, persuasiveness, and creativity (ability to think of new ways to use collected materials, for example) also will serve the future recycling coordinator well.

Exploring

Those interested in exploring a career as a recycling coordinator should start by getting familiar with the issues. Why is sorting garbage so costly? Why are some materials recycled and not others? Where are the markets? What are some creative uses for recyclable materials? You can explore what's going on both nationally and in your area. Some states have more extensive recycling programs than others; for example, some have bottle deposit laws or other innovative programs to boost recycling efforts. Get to know who's doing what and what remains to be done. Read industry-related magazines; two informative publications are *Recycling Today* and *Resource Recycling*. A useful book that focuses on environmental career possibilities is *The Complete Guide to Environmental Careers in the 21st Century*, by the Environmental Careers Organization.

Next, someone considering this field could tour a local material recovery facility and talk with the staff there. You might even volunteer to work for a recycling organization. Large and small communities frequently have groups that support recycling with fund drives and information campaigns.

Also, most municipal public meetings and workshops are good places to learn about how you can help with recycling in your community.

Employers

Recycling coordinators are almost exclusively employed by some level of government; they oversee recycling programs at the city, county, or state level. A limited number of recycling coordinators may find work with waste haulers that offer recycling coordination as part of their contracts to municipalities. Recycling coordinators work in communities of all sizes—from rural countywide programs to urban ones. When states first mandated recycling, larger counties that generated more waste generally were the first to hire recycling coordinators. However as more states set and achieve higher recycling goals, smaller cities and even rural areas need someone to coordinate their growing programs. At the state level, state environmental protection agencies or community development agencies may employ coordinators to administer state grants to and advise local recycling programs all over the state. Large organizations, such as colleges or military bases, are other employers of recycling coordinators.

Starting Out

A first job as a recycling coordinator is most likely to be with a smaller municipal program. Most colleges have a network of career referral services for their graduates, and city or county governments with openings for recycling coordinators often use these services to advertise positions to qualified graduates. Positions at the state level also may be available. Someone with previous experience with waste management projects, issues, and operations in addition to the right educational background is likely to get the more sought-after positions in larger cities and state governments. Hands-on experience can be obtained via internships, volunteering, cooperative education, summer employment, or research projects, says ECO.

Students can gain experience during summers off from college, or if necessary, after college by volunteering or serving an internship with a recycling program in their area. If internships aren't available, paid work at a waste facility is a way for students interested in recycling to earn money over the summer and learn the very basics of recycling. Volunteering for a waste management consulting firm or nonprofit environmental organization is another way to get practical experience with recyclables. Some students may benefit by looking no further than their own college. Most colleges have their own recycling programs and students may find part-time work during the school year in their own college's recycling program. Contact the physical plant operations department or student employment services at your school.

Advancement

In most cases, "recycling coordinator" is the top spot in the recycling program. Advancement isn't really an option, unless the coordinator moves to another, perhaps larger municipal program, to a private employer, or in some cases, to a different field. There is a fair amount of turnover in the field because recycling coordinator positions, in many cases, are training ground for college graduates who eventually move on to other fields where they use skills they developed as recycling coordinators. Because recycling coordinators develop so many useful skills, they often find work in related fields, such as for small business administrations and nonprofit organizations or as government administrators.

Since many states have waste-handling projects, someone with good experience at the local level might move into a state-level job—"recycling expert" is a position in some states' waste-handling departments. Opportunities with private businesses with in-house recycling needs or with solid waste management consultants or businesses might also constitute advancement. Finally, recycling coordinators also have the opportunity to expand their own programs. Through their efforts, a modest program with a limited staff and budget could blossom into a full-scale, profitable venture for the community. The coordinator could conceivably extend the scope of the program; improve links with state or local government officials, the public, and private business and industry; receive more funding; add staff; and otherwise increase the extent and prominence of the program.

Earnings

Salaries vary widely for recycling coordinators. Starting salaries range from $22,000 per year in smaller counties or cities to $40,000 and higher for coordinators in larger municipalities, according to the 1998 book by ECO,

The Complete Guide to Environmental Careers in the 21st Century. Another salary survey, conducted by the National Association of Counties in 1997, puts the average starting wage in counties with populations under 25,000 at $19,568. The average starting wage in counties with populations of 100,000 to 249,999 was $41,968. Some of the highest salaries reported were in counties with populations over 1 million, such as Maricopa County, Ariz., where the starting wage was $60,507 in 1997. Salaries vary in different regions of the country. Positions in areas with a higher cost of living, such as California, Arizona, New York, and Washington, DC, for example, tend to pay more. Benefits vary too, but most local governments offer full-time employees a good, though basic, benefit program that generally includes paid health insurance; a retirement plan; and holiday, vacation, and sick pay.

Work Environment

Recycling coordinators are essentially administrators. As such, they primarily work indoors, either in their offices, or in meetings or giving speeches. Recycling coordinators need to watch costs, understand markets, and work within budgets. They should be able to be firm with contractors when necessary. They need to demonstrate good judgment and leadership, and they may need to justify their decisions and actions to city council members or others. Stresses are part of the job, including dealing with government bureaucracy, dips in community participation, services that fall short of expectation, fluctuating markets for recyclables, and other less-than-ideal situations.

Generally, recycling coordinators work 40 hours per week if they are full time. Some positions may be part time, but for both work arrangements, working hours are generally during the day with weekends off. Occasionally, recycling coordinators may need to attend meetings in the evening, such as a county or city board meeting, or speak before a community group that meets at night. Sometimes facility or landfill tours that a recycling coordinator may arrange or participate in to generate publicity for the program may be offered on weekends. Also occasionally, recycling coordinators may leave the office setting to visit the material recovery facility, which can be noisy and dirty if compacting equipment and conveyers are running.

Outlook

The outlook for municipal recycling coordinators is excellent. According to ECO, thousands of these professionals will be needed into the early part of the 21st century, as more and more municipalities commit to full recycling programs. ECO says the job of municipal recycling coordinator is not only one of the fastest growing jobs in the environmental industry but also in any industry. As states strive to meet their increasingly ambitious waste-reduction and recycling goals, people who can make it happen on the local level are going to be crucial. Although the recycling industry is subject to business fluctuations, demand and new technologies have created a viable market for the recycled materials. Consumers generally respond favorably to buying products made from recycled goods, as long as they are quality products. With new uses and improved production of such goods, demand is expected to be steady into the next century.

Nationwide, the waste management and recycling industries will be needing more people to run recovery facilities, design new recycling technologies, come up with new ways to use recyclables, and do related work. Private businesses are also expected to hire recycling coordinators to manage in-house programs.

For More Information

For information on education and training:

Environmental Careers Organization
179 South Street
Boston, MA 02111
Tel: 617-426-4375
Web: http://www.eco.org

National Recycling Coalition
1727 King Street, Suite 105
Alexandria, VA 22314
Tel: 703-683-9025
Web: http://www.earthsystems.org

Soil Conservationists and Technicians

	School Subjects
Agriculture Biology	
	Personal Skills
Communication/ideas Helping/teaching	
	Work Environment
Indoors and outdoors Primarily multiple locations	
	Minimum Education Level
Associate's degree (soil conservationists) High school diploma (soil conservation technicians)	
	Salary Range
$15,500 to $45,200 to $70,000	
	Certification or Licensing
Voluntary	
	Outlook
About as fast as the average	

Overview

Soil conservationists develop conservation plans to help land users, such as farmers and ranchers, developers, homeowners, and government officials, best meet their land use goals while adhering to government conservation regulations. They suggest plans to conserve and reclaim soil, preserve or restore wetlands and other rare ecological areas, rotate crops for increased yields and soil conservation, reduce water pollution, and restore or increase wildlife populations. They assess the land users' needs, costs, maintenance requirements, and the life expectancy of various conservation practices. They plan design specifications using survey and field information, technical guides, and engineering field manuals. Conservationists also give talks to various organizations to educate land users and the public in general about how to conserve and restore soil and water resources. Many of their recommendations are based on information provided to them by soil scientists.

Soil conservation technicians work more directly with land users by putting the ideas and plans of the conservationist into action. In their work they use basic engineering and surveying tools, instruments, and techniques. They perform engineering surveys and design and implement conservation practices like terraces and grassed waterways. Soil conservation technicians monitor projects during and after construction, and periodically revisit the site to evaluate the practices and plans.

History

In 1908, President Theodore Roosevelt appointed a National Conservation Commission to oversee the proper conservation of the country's natural resources. As a result, many state and local conservation organizations were formed, and Americans began to take a serious interest in preserving their land's natural resources.

During World War I, farmers—who wished to capitalize on the shortage of wheat—planted many thousands of acres of wheat, mostly in Middle Western states. The crop was repeated year after year, until the soil was depleted. This depletion of the soil and the destruction of the natural cover of the land by too much cultivation led to the disastrous dust storms of the mid-1930s.

As a result of what happened in the "Dust Bowl," in 1935, Congress established the Soil Conservation Service of the U.S. Department of Agriculture. Because more than 800 million tons of topsoil had already been blown away by the winds over the plains, the job of reclaiming the land through wise conservation practices was not an easy one. In addition to the large areas of the Middle West which had become desert land, there were other badly eroded lands throughout the country.

Fortunately, emergency planning came to the aid of the newly established Soil Conservation Service. The Civilian Conservation Corps (CCC) was created to help alleviate unemployment during the Great Depression of the 1930s. The CCC established camps in rural areas and assigned people to aid in many different kinds of conservation. Soil conservationists directed those portions of the CCC program designed to halt the loss of topsoil by wind and water action.

Much progress has been made in the years since the Soil Conservation Service was established. Wasted land has been reclaimed and further loss has been prevented. Land-grant colleges have initiated programs to help farmers understand the principles and procedures of soil conservation. The Cooperative Research, Education and Extension Service (within the

Department of Agriculture) provides workers who are skilled in soil conservation to work with these programs.

Throughout the United States today there are several thousand federally appointed soil conservation districts. A worker employed by the government works in a particular district to demonstrate soil conservation to farmers and agricultural businesses. There are usually one or more professional soil conservationists and one or more soil conservation technicians working in each district.

The Job

Soil conservationists and technicians with the federal Soil Conservation Service help scientists and engineers obtain preliminary data used to establish and maintain soil and water conservation plans. They may also work closely with landowners and operators to establish and maintain sound conservation practices in land management and use.

Conservationists oversee soil conservation technicians who assist with preliminary engineering surveys; lay out contours, terraces, tile drainage systems, and irrigation systems; plant grasses and trees; collect soil samples and gather information from field notes; improve woodlands; assist in farm pond design and management; make maps from aerial photographs; and inspect specific areas to determine conservation needs.

Some conservationists and technicians work for the Bureau of Land Management which oversees hundreds of millions of acres of public domain. Workers in this federal agency help survey publicly owned areas, and pinpoint land features to determine the best use of public lands. They may be called upon to supervise a four- to six-person surveying team in carrying out the actual survey.

Soil conservation technicians in the Bureau of Reclamation serve as assistants to civil, construction, materials, or general engineers. Their job is to oversee certain phases of such projects as the construction of dams, and irrigation planning. The Bureau's ultimate goal is the control of water and soil resources for the benefit of farm, home, and city.

The following short paragraphs describe some positions typically held by entry-level soil conservationists and technicians.

Range technicians work closely with *range conservationists* helping to manage rangeland, most of which is in the western part of the United States. They determine the value of rangeland, its grazing capabilities, erosion hazards, and livestock potential.

Physical science technician aides gather data in the field, studying the physical characteristics of the soil, mapping land, and producing aerial survey maps for use by soil conservationists.

Engineering technician aides conduct field tests and oversee some phases of construction on dams and irrigation projects. They manage water resources and perform soil-conservation services. They also measure acreage, place property boundaries, and define drainage areas on maps.

Cartographic survey technician aides work with cartographers (map makers) to survey the public domain, setting boundaries, pinpointing land features, and determining the most beneficial public use.

The following short paragraphs describe some of the positions held by more experienced soil conservationists and technicians.

Cartographic technicians perform technical work in mapping or charting the earth or graphically representing geographical information.

Geodetic technicians perform nonprofessional work in the analysis, evaluation, processing, computation, and selection of geodetic survey data. (Geodesy is the science of determining the size and shape of the earth, the intensity and direction of the force of gravity, and the elevation of points on or near the earth's surface.)

Physical science technicians help professional scientists calibrate and operate measuring instruments; mix solutions; make routine chemical analyses; and set up and operate test apparatus.

Surveying technicians perform surveys to conduct field measurement and mapping, to lay out construction, to check the accuracy of dredging operations, or to provide reference points and lines for related work. They gather data for the design of highways and dams, or the construction of topographic maps or nautical and aeronautical charts.

Range conservationists administer and operate range conservation programs to properly conserve, develop, and utilize ranges and rangeland; to provide for the conservation, management, and utilization of related resources; and to stabilize the livestock industry, which depends upon the range for its existence.

Requirements

High School

While in high school, prospective conservationists and technicians should take at least one year of algebra, enough English to be articulate and convincing in speech and writing, and one year of biology. For technicians who anticipate that they may work in areas of soil conservation involving contact with farmers and ranchers, high school courses in vocational agriculture are strongly recommended.

Postsecondary Training

The federal government requires soil conservationists to earn at least 30 college credit hours and significant work experience in order to be considered for a position. A bachelor's degree in agronomy, agricultural education, range management, forestry, or agricultural engineering will be especially helpful to the aspiring soil conservationist. Some conservationists may consider earning a master's degree in a natural resources field. A college education is not required of soil conservation technicians.

Typical first-year courses in a two-year postsecondary program include such courses as applied mathematics, communication skills, basic soils, botany, chemistry, zoology, and introduction to range management. Typical second-year courses include American government, surveying, forestry, game management, soil and water conservation, economics, fish management, and soil and water conservation engineering.

Conservationists and technicians must have some practical experience in the use of soil conservation techniques before they enter the field. Therefore, a good part of their postsecondary education includes on-the-job training.

Certification or Licensing

No certification or license is required of soil conservationists and technicians. Employment by government agencies is usually based on a competitive examination. The American Society of Agronomy and the Soil and Water Conservation Society offer certification in soil science.

Other Requirements

Soil conservationists and technicians must be able to apply practical as well as theoretical knowledge to their work. They need to have a working knowledge of soil and water characteristics; be skilled in management of woodlands, wildlife areas, and recreation areas; and have a knowledge of surveying instruments and practices, mapping, and the procedures used for interpreting aerial photographs.

Soil conservationists and technicians should also be able to write clear, concise reports to demonstrate and explain the results of their tests, studies, and recommendations. It goes without saying that a love for the outdoors and an appreciation for all natural resources are essential for success and personal fulfillment in this job.

Exploring

One of the best ways for you to become acquainted with soil conservation work and technology is through summer or part-time work on a farm. Other ways to explore this career include joining a 4-H Club or the Future Farmers of America (FFA). Science courses that include lab sections, and mathematics courses that focus on practical problem solving will also help give you a feel for this kind of work.

Employers

Most soil conservationists and technicians work for the federal government, specifically for the Soil Conservation Service, the Bureau of Land Management, and the Bureau of Reclamation. Others work for agencies at the state and county level. Soil conservationists and technicians also work for private agencies and firms such as banks and loan agencies, mining or steel companies, and public utilities companies.

Starting Out

Most students in a two-year technical institute gain work experience by working a summer job in their areas of interest. Students can get information on summer positions through their schools' placement offices. Often, contacts made on summer jobs lead to permanent employment after graduation. In addition, college placement officers and faculty members are frequently valuable sources of advice and information in finding employment.

Most soil conservationists and technicians find work with state, county, or federal agencies. Specific details of the application procedure for these jobs vary according to the level of government in which the technician is seeking work. In general, however, students begin the application procedure during the fourth semester of their programs and should expect some form of competitive examination as part of the process. College placement personnel can help students find out about the details of application procedures. Representatives of government agencies frequently visit college campuses to explain employment possibilities to students and sometimes to recruit for their agencies.

Advancement

Soil conservationists and technicians may continue their education while working by taking additional courses at night at a local college or technical institute. Federal agencies that employ conservationists and technicians have a policy of "promotion from within." Because of this policy, there is a continuing opportunity for such workers to advance through the ranks. The degree of advancement that all conservationists and technicians can expect in their working careers is determined by their aptitudes, abilities, and of course their desire to advance.

Earnings

The majority of soil conservationists and technicians work for the federal government, and their salaries are determined by their government service rating. In 1997, the average annual salary for soil conservationists employed by the federal government was $45,200, according to the *Occupational*

Outlook Handbook. Those with bachelor's degrees started at $19,500 or $24,200 a year depending on academic achievement; with a master's degree, $24,200 or $29,600; and with a doctorate, $35,800. The salaries of workers employed by state and local governments vary widely depending on the state or county for which they work.

The salaries of conservationists and technicians working for private firms or agencies will be roughly comparable to the earnings of other similarly trained agricultural technicians employed by private firms. In general, conservationists in this area receive beginning salaries of $19,800 a year. Those with a grade point average of at least 3.0 or who have a master's degree with two years work experience may earn a starting salary of $22,000 per year. Those conservationists with considerable experience who have gained consistent promotion can earn from $40,000 to $49,500 or more a year. Conservationists who have management responsibilities may earn as much as $65,000 to $70,000 a year. Soil conservation technicians, who do not usually have a college degree, earn starting salaries of $15,500; top pay for this position reaches $20,000 per year.

Work Environment

Soil conservationists and technicians usually work 40 hours per week, except in unusual or emergency situations. They have opportunities to travel, and in some positions with federal agencies, they may travel frequently.

Soil conservation is an outdoor job. Conservation workers travel to work sites by car, but they must often walk great distances to the problem area. Although they sometimes work from aerial photographs and other on-site pictures, they cannot work from pictures alone. They must visit the spot that presents the problem in order to make appropriate recommendations.

Although soil conservationists and technicians spend much of their working time outdoors, office work is also necessary when generating detailed reports of their work to agency offices.

In their role as assistants to professionals, soil conservation technicians often assume the role of public relations representatives of the government to landowners and land managers. They must be able to explain the underlying principles of the structures that they design and the surveys that they perform.

To meet these and other requirements of the job, conservationists and technicians should be prepared to continue their education both formally and informally throughout their careers. They must stay aware of current periodicals and studies to keep up to date in their areas of specialization.

Soil conservationists and technicians gain satisfaction from knowing that theirs is a vitally important job to the economy of the nation. Without their work, large portions of land in the United States could become barren within a generation.

Outlook

Most soil conservationists and technicians are employed by the federal government; therefore, employment opportunities will depend in large part on levels of government spending. It is always difficult to predict future government policies; however, this is an area where the need for government involvement is apparent and pressing. The vast majority of America's cropland has suffered from some sort of erosion, and only continued efforts by soil conservation professionals can prevent a dangerous depletion of our most valuable resource—fertile soil.

Some soil conservationists and technicians are employed by public utility companies, banks and loan agencies, state and local governments, and mining or steel companies. At present, a relatively small number of soil conservation workers are employed by these firms or agencies. However, decreased levels of employment by the federal government could lead to increased employment in these areas.

For More Information

For information on soil conservation careers and certification, contact:

American Society of Agronomy
Career Development and Placement Service
677 South Segoe Road
Madison, WI 53711
Tel: 608-273-8080
Email: headquarters@Agronomy.org
Web: http://www.agronomy.org

For information on careers in soil conservation and certification, contact:

Soil and Water Conservation Society
7515 NE Ankeny Road
Ankeny, IA 50021
Tel: 515-289-2331
Web: http://www.swcs.org/

For information on government soil conservation careers, contact:

Natural Resources Conservation Service
U.S. Department of Agriculture
Attn: Conservation Communications Staff
PO Box 2890
Washington, DC 20013
Web: http://www.nrcs.usda.gov/

Soil Scientists

Agriculture Earth science	School Subjects
Leadership/management Technical/scientific	Personal Skills
Indoors and outdoors Primarily multiple locations	Work Environment
Bachelor's degree	Minimum Education Level
$26,000 to $49,000 to $87,000+	Salary Range
Voluntary	Certification or Licensing
About as fast as the average	Outlook

Overview

Soil scientists study the physical, chemical, and biological characteristics and behaviors of soils. They determine the origin, distribution, composition, and classification of soils so that they may be put to the most productive and effective use.

History

As recently as 200 years ago, no one suspected soil could be depleted by constant use. When crops were poor, everything was blamed except the soil in which they were grown. In some parts of the world, mysterious or supernatural forces are still considered responsible for poor harvests.

Soil is one of our most important natural resources. Like air, however, soil is often taken for granted until its condition becomes too bad to ignore. An increasing population, moreover, has made the United States conscious of the fact that its welfare is dependent upon fertile soil capable of producing food for hundreds of millions of people.

Soil is formed by the breaking of rocks and the decay of trees, plants, and animals. It may take as long as 500 years to make just one inch of topsoil. Unwise and wasteful farming methods can destroy that inch of soil in just a few short years.

Each rainstorm may carry thousands of pounds of precious topsoil away. Rains also dissolve the chemicals in unprotected soils, making it more difficult to grow healthy crops. Erosion has been a problem of major proportions in the United States, but soil scientists and soil conservationists have made some progress at halting it.

It was not until approximately 130 years ago that agriculture was considered important enough to deserve the attention of the federal government. In May 1862, the U.S. Department of Agriculture was formed. Its primary purpose at the time was to give farmers information about new crops and new farming techniques. Although the Department of Agriculture started as a small undertaking, it has become one of the largest agencies of the federal government, despite the fact that there are only half as many farmers in this country as there were 100 years ago.

The 1933 Agricultural Adjustment Act inaugurated a policy of giving direct government aid to farmers. The Soil Conservation Service was established two years later. This service developed as a direct result of the disastrous dust storms of the mid-1930s, which blew away millions of tons of valuable topsoil and destroyed fertile cropland throughout the midwestern states. Because of the efforts of the scientists employed by the Soil Conservation Service, much of this ruined land has been reclaimed.

Since 1937, all 50 states, in cooperation with the Department of Agriculture, have organized themselves into soil conservation districts. The department sends soil scientists and soil conservationists to help farmers within each district establish and maintain farming practices that will use land in the wisest possible ways.

The Job

Soil scientists do much of their work outdoors. They must tramp over fields, confer with farmers, give advice on crop rotation or fertilizers, assess the amount of field drainage, and take soil samples. They advise farmers about proper cover crops to protect bare earth from the ravages of the wind and weather.

Soil scientists may also specialize in one particular aspect of the work. For example, they may work as a *soil mapper* or *soil surveyor*. These specialists study soil structure, origin, and capabilities through field observations, laboratory examinations, and controlled experimentation. Their investigations are aimed at determining the most suitable uses for a particular soil.

Soil fertility experts develop practices that will increase or maintain productivity. They test the soils chemically and conduct field investigations to determine the relation of soil acidity to plant growth. They also relate the use of various fertilizers and other soil additives to local soil characteristics; to tillage, crop rotation, and other farm practices; and to the requirements of particular crops.

All soil scientists work in the laboratory. They make chemical analyses of the soil and examine soil samples under the microscope to determine bacterial and plant-food components. They write reports that are drawn from their field notes and from the samples of soil that they have analyzed.

Soil science is part of the science of agronomy, which also encompasses crop science. Soil and crop scientists work together in agricultural experiment stations during all seasons, doing research on crop production, soil fertility, and various kinds of soil management.

Some soil and crop scientists travel to remote sections of the world in search of plants and grasses that may thrive in this country and contribute to our food supply, pasture land, or soil replenishing efforts. Some crop scientists go overseas to advise farmers in other countries on how to treat their soils. A number of soil scientists with advanced degrees teach in colleges of agriculture. Many who teach also conduct research projects.

Requirements

High School

If you're interested in pursuing a career in agronomy or soil science, you should follow your high school's college preparatory course. Mathematics and science, as well as English and public speaking, are essential courses. A person needs to be able to speak persuasively and effectively to become a convincing soil scientist. Report writing is also an important part of the job.

Postsecondary Training

A bachelor's degree in agronomy or soil science is the minimum educational requirement to become a soil scientist. Physics, geology, bacteriology, botany, chemistry, soil and plant morphology, soil fertility, soil classification, and soil genesis are all requirements for the prospective soil scientist.

Most colleges of agriculture also offer masters' and doctoral degrees in agronomy or soil science. To direct and administer research programs, soil scientists usually need doctoral degrees. The same is true for those seeking teaching positions at the university level. Master's degrees are helpful for many research positions.

Certification or Licensing

Soil scientists may seek to be listed in the American Registry of Certified Professionals in Agronomy, Crops, and Soils. To qualify for this, they must earn a bachelor's degree and work five years in the field. Those with advanced degrees can qualify with less experience.

Other Requirements

It's good to have some farm experience or background before going into soil science. You should be able to work effectively alone and with others on projects. You must have good communication skills in order to explain your findings. Computer skills are becoming increasingly important; you'll need an understanding of word processing, the Internet, multimedia software, databases, and possibly even programming languages. You will have to spend many hours outdoors in all kinds of weather, so you must be able to endure difficult and uncomfortable physical conditions.

Exploring

If you live in an agricultural community, you should be able to find some opportunities for part-time or summer work on a farm or ranch. A Future Farmers of America (FFA) program will introduce you to the concerns of farmers and researchers. A local 4-H club can also give you valuable experience in agriculture. Contact your county's soil conservation department, and other government agencies, to learn about regional projects.

Employers

Most soil scientists work for state or federal departments of agriculture. However, soil scientists are also employed by such private business firms as fertilizer companies, where they may engage in research work to improve the product or engage in sales work to increase the use of the product. Soil scientists may be employed by private research laboratories, real estate firms, or land appraisal boards. They may work for state road departments to determine the quality and condition of the soil over which roads will be built. Other soil scientists may work as private consultants for bankers and other clients who are engaged in making loans on property. Some soil consultants work for park departments or for farm management agencies.

Starting Out

College graduates with degrees in agronomy or soil science should apply directly to the Resources Conservation Service of the Department of Agriculture, the Department of the Interior, the Environmental Protection Agency, or the appropriate state government agency. University placement services generally have listings for specific openings.

Private employers of soil scientists include agricultural service companies, banks, insurance and real estate firms, food products companies, wholesale distributors, and environmental and engineering consulting companies. Some public employers of soil scientists, other than the federal, state, and local governments, are land appraisal boards, experimental stations, land-grant colleges and universities, conservation departments, and Cooperative Extension agencies. Soil scientists who work overseas may be employed by the U.S. Agency for International Development.

Advancement

Salary increases are the most common form of advancement for soil scientists. The nature of the job may not change appreciably even after many years of service. There is, of course, always the possibility of advancement into positions of greater responsibility. Administrative and supervisory positions, however, are few in comparison with the number of jobs that must be done in the field. Those who go on to obtain graduate degrees may anticipate moving into more responsible positions, especially in soil research.

For those soil scientists engaged in college teaching, an advanced degree may well mean an advancement in academic rank and responsibility. For soil scientists employed by private business firms, there may be the opportunity to advance into positions such as department head or research director. Advancement to supervisory positions or other positions of responsibility is also possible in such state agencies as road departments.

Earnings

According to the U.S. Department of Labor, the average pay for soil scientists in 1997 was $49,400 a year. Soil scientists working for the government can enter the field at GS-7 (regulated government pay scale) which is between $26,000 and $35,000 a year. But government grade level and starting salary depend on experience, education, and grade point average. Those with doctorates and a great deal of experience may be qualified for GS-14, which is between $67,000 and $87,000. Unless you're hired for just a short-term research project, you are likely to receive health and retirement benefits in addition to your annual salary.

Work Environment

Most soil scientists work 40 hours a week. Their work is varied, ranging from field work to the work of examining samples of soil and constructing detailed maps that must be done in the laboratory. Some jobs may involve travel—even to foreign countries—and some may include teaching responsibilities or the supervision of training programs in the field.

Outlook

The career of soil scientist will be affected by USDA and Environmental Protection Agency involvement in farming studies. Technological advances, such as computer programs and new methods of conservation, will allow scientists to better protect the environment as well as improve farm production. One of the challenges facing future soil scientists will be convincing farmers to change their current methods of tilling and chemical treatment in favor of environmentally safer methods.

Soil scientists will be able to better evaluate soils and plants with new, more precise research methods. Combine-mounted yield monitors will produce data as the farmer crosses the field, and satellites will provide more detailed field information. With computer images, scientists will also be able to examine plant roots more carefully.

For More Information

For a career resources booklet, contact SSSA, or visit its Web site.

Soil Science Society of America
677 South Segoe Road
Madison, WI 53711
Tel: 608-273-8095
Web: http://www.soils.org

For information about membership, seminars, and issues affecting soil scientists, visit the NSCSS Web site, or contact:

National Society of Consulting Soil Scientists
325 Pennsylvania Avenue, SE, Suite 700
Washington DC 20003
Tel: 800-535-7148
Web: http://www.nscss.org

Index